When
SACRIFICE
is Gain

Tim Maddocks

ISBN: 9798326425515

THE NAKED MAN CARRYING A CROSS

The greatest motivation for living is a cause valued enough to sacrifice all for. Jesus, the Son of God, had just such a cause: the salvation of sin-infested humanity. To the average extra-terrestrial onlooker, Jesus' cause seemed a hopeless investment of heaven's very best resources. But for Jesus, the possibility of granting man victory over sin and death made the ultimate sacrifice, death on a cross, worth the investment. For Christians, the cross has become the symbol of living and dying for such a cause.

After Jesus' resurrection He extended an invitation to His followers to accept His cause as their cause, saying, "Peace be with you; as my Father has sent Me, I send you." John 20:21. Jesus' words recorded in Luke 9:23 incorporate the cross symbolism into this invitation: "If any man will come after me, let him deny himself, and take up his cross daily, and follow me." Jesus' sacrifice of His life would result in the salvation of an innumerable multitude. This is by far the best example of 'When Sacrifice is Gain.'

The cover picture of the naked man represents the follower of Jesus who has surrendered all he is, and all he has to make way for Jesus to clothe him in His own righteousness. The cross symbolises his belief that "Greater love has no man than to lay down his life for his friends" John 15:13. By taking up the cross, he has accepted Jesus' invitation to join Jesus in the ultimate cause, that of the salvation of humanity. His walking position signifies that he is on a journey. While Jesus is not visibly with him, he is constantly aware of Jesus' presence for he has Jesus' promise recorded in Matthew 28:20, "I am with you always, even to the end of the age."

The white background is an expression of the joy and peace that the sojourner with Jesus experiences. The blue colour of the letters symbolises that as children of God we are royalty granted to reign for eternity with Him. When you become the naked man with the cross, you too will realise that sacrifice truly is gain.

WHERE THANKS IS DUE

The writing of this short book is only possible because God saw potential in us that we could not see in ourselves. God chose us, trained us, forgave us, and laboured together with us to take His dream for what could be and make it what it is today. God's patience with us, never giving up on us when we messed up, has taught us much about His love for us and the people He wants to save. This story is about God and how He has shaped our lives while working through us to shape the lives of others. All praise belongs to Him.

This little book highlights selected events of 39 years of mission, but it is told through my eyes. Wendy, my best earthly friend and beloved wife of 41 years, has been with me throughout this journey, experiencing the joys, hardships and blessings. I daily thank God for choosing her to be my partner in mission. Without her there would be no story to tell.

I am grateful to my children, Caleb, Shannon and Ly, who have stuck with us through a life of mission despite during their childhood seeing their parents so involved in the Lord's work that they sometimes felt neglected.

We praise God for parents that never complained about only seeing their children and grandchildren for a week or two every two or three years, and for their financial contributions to the mission.

Many people who have played important roles in this story are not mentioned, but they are not forgotten: prayer warriors, financial supporters, volunteers and our

Cambodian brothers and sisters in Christ who have partnered together with God and us.

I am also grateful to the leaders of all levels of the Seventh-day Adventist Church who have encouraged us in word and action to be faithful to the Lord's calling on our lives.

I am grateful and indebted to the many people who read through the draft copies of this book and made editorial suggestions.

As you read this book, it is my prayer, that God will open your eyes to the unique calling He has for your lives, if you are not already living it. I truly believe that now, like no other time in this earth's history, we are to die to self, giving God the space to live out His life within us. Now is the time for God's people to unite as one, making Jesus, King of Kings, known to all the world. This story highlights what God will do when He has our complete cooperation.

TIm Maddocks
April, 2024

CONTENTS

Every Journey Has a Beginning

Wendy and I (Tim) had secretly engaged at the ages of 15 and 16. Wendy was in grade 11 and I was in grade 12. I had chosen the drinking water fountain outside the library at Carmel Adventist College in Western Australia as the romantic spot to propose to Wendy. Choir practise had just finished and we were on our way to evening library study period. We had met seven months earlier, and we had fallen in love.

That same year, Pastor Bob Possingham, our Union Youth Director, held a week of Spiritual emphasis. Forty three years later, two short sentences of his are still ringing in my ears, "Come see a man", and "Didn't he want it". After coming to Christ at seven years of age, thanks to an archaeological evangelistic series preached by Pastor Athol Tolhurst, I loved the Lord, but during that week of spiritual emphasis the Holy Spirit got a hold of both Wendy and my hearts. The invitation to 'come see a man' is the invitation we have spent our lives offering to others.

We were sold out to each other and sold out to the Lord but Laedocian at heart. Our relationship and life goals had been shaped by the Australian society we lived in. We were intrinsically self centred with personal goals that failed to incorporate Jesus' request to 'Go make disciples'. We were honoured to be disciples but really had no comprehension of what responsibilities came with the title.

Wendy and I were married in Busselton, Western Australia, on my 19th birthday, Wendy was 18 and everything I could wish for as a soul mate, but little did

either of us realise on our marriage day the adventure
God had in mind for the two of us.

Re-programmed For Mission

As newlyweds, we settled into married life in our rented apartment in the city of Perth, Western Australia. Both of us were studying our chosen careers at university, Wendy in the field of Podiatry and I in Biology. We saw ourselves finishing university and settling into life in Western Australia. In all our prayers and commitments to God, we had failed to ask God what were His aspirations for our lives. God was about to intervene.

While enjoying doing research in the Australian desert with one of my professors during vacation time, God took advantage of a conversation to make a radical change in my life goals. My professor and a fellow student were talking about the student's decision to add to his Biology degree a graduate diploma in Education so that he could follow a teaching career. The idea of being a teacher had never entered my mind, but at that moment, I heard the voice of God say very clearly to me, 'You are to be a teacher.' It was profound and life changing. I together with my fellow student took the one year graduate diploma in Secondary Education, setting my life on the path of a teacher.

A second intervention happened when Carmel College, our alma mater, put on a library sale, cleaning out their shelves of old books. Wendy and I found ourselves looking through books and going home with a stack of mission story books which we decided to read together as our evening worship activity. With each succeeding book, the Holy Spirit worked on our world view, taking us from a self centred view of the world that focussed around what we desired, to a world view that had Christ in the centre and partnership with Him as the driving

1

force. We read stories from Africa, India, China, South-East Asia, Papua New Guinea, South America, and the Pacific Islands, stories of valiant missionaries who were willing to sacrifice everything to take the gospel to the world. Our personal vision for our lives was beginning to look like a life of boredom compared to what these missionaries of old lived and died!

At some point along this journey, we both came to the conclusion that missions was our calling. At the ages of 19 and 20, we made the three fold commitment to go anywhere, do anything, for any length of time with our Lord. Later we added at any cost, although I think unconsciously that commitment was already made.

With only months left before we would both complete our university studies, we decided to apply to the General Conference of the Seventh-day Adventist Church for volunteer work. We made it clear that we would go anywhere, do anything, for any length of time. Remuneration was not a factor. We waited patiently, expectantly for our assignment to work with God for the salvation of souls. Finally the long awaited letter arrived in the mail box, and we were in for a surprise.

We knew that God had sent out the two delivered demoniacs as missionaries despite them having only hours of preparation (Mark5:1-20). We had spent years getting our education. The letter was short, thanking us for our application but declining our offer to serve God on the grounds that we had no experience. That was 1984. Confused, but believing mission was God's calling for our lives, we wrote to a pastor in Papua New Guinea to ask if he had mission work we could do. This time the letter was positive, offering us work eight hours hike up into the mountains of Papua New Guinea. Believing this was where God wanted us, we wrote confirming we would go and began making the necessary preparations. Often an open door is mistaken as God's will being confirmed. I don't remember asking God if this was His calling for our lives. We just assumed it was. Weeks passed, preparation was well underway when God mysteriously intervened. The door was not shut but another door opened.

I was visiting Carmel College where I had recently done my final session of practice teaching. The school secretary received a phone call from the Western Australian Conference of the Seventh-day Adventist Church executive secretary asking if she knew how to contact Tim Maddocks. Wendy and I were poor students supported by the government of Australia and did not have a telephone in our rented apartment. I think that the secretary was surprised by the timing of the phone call, knowing that at any other time she would not have known how to contact me except by mail. Divine providence was at work. I also was surprised by the news that the conference secretary wanted to talk with me. I had never met him before and had no idea as to why he would be calling. Minutes later, I was talking to the conference secretary and learning of another door to mission service, this one as a science teacher in Samoa with a salary. The offer came with a condition, I had to reply within 24 hours. I hastened to the university to find Wendy and talk and pray together about this unplanned turn of events. We had set our hearts on serving in Papua New Guinea.

We had made God a promise: go anywhere, do anything, for any length of time. The call was not the problem, money was not a lure, but now what was important was knowing God's will. This time we made no hasty decision, but chose to wait on the Lord. That evening we opened the mission story book to where the bookmark lay, and began to read a story about a country we had not previously discovered in our mission story adventures, the country of Samoa, the same country that only hours before we had been called to serve. God's will was now made clear by providence. It was not by chance that the conference secretary called Carmel College at the very time I was visiting. Nor was it by chance that we were called to Samoa the very day the mission story was about Samoa. I don't know how God engineered that double providence but I am sure He did, and as a result our lives were about to begin a unique journey which is still ongoing 39 years later.

Samoan Journey Begins

Early January, 1985, we boarded a plane leaving Western Australia. This was the beginning of our missionary journey. Our minds were full of the stories of amazing missionaries, many of whom had willingly sacrificed their lives to make Jesus known. Now it was our turn. We were young, 20 and 21 years of age, idealistic and naive. Based on the stories of missionaries, many of whom were long gone, we had formulated our picture of what constituted the ideal missionary. We were going to live among the people, like the people, eating their food, dressing like them, learning their culture and becoming a part of it. The words we used to describe this lifestyle were "going native".

Samoa bound, we made a stop over in Sydney, Australia, to attend a missionary orientation training at the South Pacific Division of the General Conference of Seventh-day Adventists Headquarters. Much useful information was gained, especially with regard to how the worldwide church works and the policies that guide it, but one thing that was taught clashed violently with our picture of the ideal missionary. All of us new missionaries were told that we should retain our own culture and not go native. Our picture of the ideal missionary was apparently a picture of a misguided missionary. It would be many years before we would finally resolve this tension and redefine the ideal missionary as incarnational: following the example of Jesus, ministering to people while living as one of them.

Personally, I have always been someone not concerned enough about planning, being happy to work things out on the fly. That became evident on our arrival to Samoa.

We arrived in a new country with no phone number for the mission, no address, only the knowledge that we would be picked up at the airport and taken to the mission compound in Apia, the capital of Western Samoa. What we had not anticipated was a cyclone that would delay our plane 12 hours, resulting in our airport pickup not knowing our revised arrival time. It was early afternoon when our plane landed on a hot, rain-soaked tarmac. Our arrival in the tropics greeted us with the very best the tropics could offer: a sauna as big as the runway. Being unused to the humidity we found breathing difficult. Clearing Immigration we went to look for the gracious person who would pick us up, but they were not to be found, no fault of theirs of course. So we found a place where we could observe the people and waited two hours. A kind lady bus driver seeing us waiting came to tell us that hers was the last bus out that day, and we were welcome to ride. She asked where we wanted to go, to which we replied, the Samoan Adventist Mission, and it was at the mission gates where she dropped us off. Our Samoan journey had begun.

We soon found ourselves in the home of the Mission President, Pastor Ripine Rimoni and recipients of the gracious hospitality of his wife. During the few days we stayed at the Samoan Mission compound, Mrs Rimoni gave us our first lessons on Samoan food. We quickly fell in love with the graciousness of the people and their food. Inspired by the food we ate in those first few days on Samoan soil, and our desire to go native, we visited the market to stock up on food in preparation for our departure to Kosena College, 50 km away, on the other side of the mountain. Avocados, coconuts, papaya, taro, all new foods to us, filled our coconut leaf basket. "Going native," here we come.

Kosena College One of Our Training Grounds

We had been informed by the General Conference of the Seventh-day Adventist Church that we had no experience, which was true, but thanks be to God that He had a plan to place us at Kosena College. There we would serve with our Samoan colleagues under two different principals, Brian Mercer and Vic Bonetti. God sent us to Samoa to begin gaining the experiences that He would later use for His glory in Cambodia.

We arrived at Kosena College in late January 1985. The College had been built ten years earlier by valiant missionaries, local workers, and students with a goal of putting Adventist Education principles into action. Our first lesson learned at the college was one of expectations. We had previously lived in a small, one bedroom, rented apartment and had been prepared to live in a thatched house in Papua New Guinea. With God's change in plans, we arrived at Kosena and were taken to our new home across the oval from the school, a modest three bedroom house raised off the ground with parking and laundry underneath. A passionfruit vine had taken over the front steps and had to be pushed back in order to ascend the stairs. The house had lots of windows overlooking the school, and beyond that the forest and mountains. We did not notice the mildew growing on the walls or the cockroaches that had been keeping the home inhabited in the absence of humans. To us this was a mansion with a view, far beyond our expectations. We noticed a sense of nervousness on our host's faces as we were introduced to the new home and a sense of relief when they saw our pleasure with the place God had provided. Apparently the previous missionaries took one look at the home with its resident cockroaches, returned to Apia city, bought tickets back to their home country and left.

During the past 39 years of mission life in the tropics, I have seen many people literally freak out at the sight of God's awesome and wonderfully made creatures which include spiders as big as small birds, foot long centipedes, scorpions, squadrons of mosquitos, and snakes of all sizes and colours. In Luke 10:19, Jesus said, "Behold, I give unto you power to tread on serpents and scorpions, and over all the power of the enemy: and nothing shall by any means hurt you." The spiritual application to this we will discuss later, but what is important to note here is a very down to earth promise of God that if taken seriously should take away the fear factor when meeting God's creatures. Today most missionaries work in big cities and for the most part don't have opportunity to appreciate God's creatures close up. Wendy and I refer to these creatures in our home as 'Living Art' which is dynamic and constantly changing. The tree frog on the living room wall, the Tokay (a foot long Gecko) walking around upside down on the kitchen ceiling, the miniature dinosaurs (skinks) proudly sunning themselves in the bedroom. The large spider on the shower curtain watching us take a shower. As missionaries we count it a privilege to get a taste of what life was like for Adam and Eve in the garden of Eden, with the difference being we have a roof over our heads.

Revelling in our new home with a view, we began to settle into mission life and the lessons it had to teach us. In the few days we had been in Samoa we had already fallen in love with the use of coconut cream in Samoan cooking. In the market we had bought a basket of husked coconuts with the goal of making coconut cream and learning how to cook with it. It quickly became apparent that once again the General Conference Volunteers department were right, we had no experience. Neither of us knew how to extract coconut cream from a coconut. Thankfully our Samoan colleagues came to our rescue providing us with the equipment and skills necessary to master this art. We, the foreign missionaries, had to be helped by the very people we had come to help. And it wouldn't be the last time either.

Several months into our first year of mission life, a wise Solomon Islander came to stay with us for a few days to get a break away from his agricultural studies at the Agricultural University in Apia. After observing us, he took me aside and asked if he could give me some advice to which I appreciatively agreed. We went for a walk and he talked with this wise 21 year old caucasian male with a university degree and graduate diploma. He appreciated that as a Westerner I had given up much to come and help the Samoan people, then recommended that I, the teacher, be teachable. He talked about the Samoan people and the valuable experience and knowledge that they had to offer. He assured me that if I would learn from them, life in their country would be so much more rewarding for everyone concerned. I have long since forgotten his name, but the wisdom he shared with me during that short walk has blessed me again and again. I realised that as an educated white man in a foreign country, I was actually a student with much to learn about life skills, other cultures and how to interact effectively and appreciatively with the people I had come to serve. We had aspired to go native, but to do so we needed to be ready to be taught by the natives. Jesus

Himself learned the language, culture and skills of the Israelite people in order to effectively witness to the people He lived among. To live incarnationally, the pride of our culture had to be subdued in order to appreciate the culture of the people we lived among.

An Adventist school that follows the True Education model is to be as self-sufficient as possible. The founders of Kosena College had that goal in mind when they established plantations, root crop gardens and a vegetable garden at the school. Kosena was a boarding school and after the school day finished the students together with the teachers worked on the grounds, gardens and general upkeep of the school. As science teacher, I was appointed to lead the students in vegetable production. The school brought in dry food goods, but fresh food was all grown on campus. Kosena was a unique growing environment with more than 200 inches of rain a year. Five days without rain was considered a drought. God in His foresight had put me in charge of tropical vegetable production to teach me agriculture the hard way. Many years would pass before I would understand God's strategic planning to equip me with skills that would later be used as the excuse to plant our family in Cambodia. Wendy with her podiatry training, was the natural choice to appoint as school nurse. Again God was working strategically, equipping her with skills that would later become invaluable in soul winning in Cambodia, but back then we were ignorant of this, willing participants in whatever activities we were asked to do and some that we created ourselves.

As a city boy, I had never driven a tractor before, let alone one with a mower on the back. In that first week on campus the local staff asked me to take the tractor to mow the campus lawns in preparation for school starting. Thirty-eight years later, I am still using that skill acquired in the mission field. It is now very apparent that while our initial rejection for volunteer work was made on our lack of experience, without going to the mission field we were unlikely to gain the experience that was needed to be successful missionaries. In mission minded circles it is common to hear the phrase, "God doesn't call the equipped, He equips the called."

Another lesson that we learned in the first year of life at Kosena was that knowledge does not trounce accountability. Let me explain. Wendy was school nurse using the medical background she had to treat the students who were sick. One evening during a study period while the principal Brian Mercer was on duty, I took him to task for over-riding decisions Wendy was making with regard to the medical care of our students. It is worthwhile mentioning that Brian was our English teacher for grades 11 and 12, so five years later, on Samoan soil, we were already well acquainted. That evening Brian taught me a very useful lesson: the person at the top is ultimately accountable. Wendy was school nurse, I was science and mathematics teacher, Brian was principal. If a student got dangerously sick or worse, died, because of a medical condition that happened on campus, Brian was responsible, not Wendy, the school nurse, nor I, the science teacher. God needed to teach me this lesson, knowing that one day, I would be the man at the top, the man who would be held accountable and therefore as leader I would sometimes have to veto decisions made by my staff even though those decisions were made in good faith and knowledge. At the youthful age of 21 years I was guilty of thinking my decisions were always right. Praise God that I have since learnt that wisdom comes with experience, and experience is not gained out of a textbook.

Working at a school where English was the required language, we had not made much effort to learn the Samoan language. During the third year of our stay in Samoa, Kosena College was closed due to low student enrolment. The school was reopened at the old campus on the Mission compound in Apia, the capital city. We relocated to the mission compound and began attending church services at the Apia Seventh-day Adventist Church, where services were held in the Samoan language. Here we experienced a frustration that many missionaries are subject to, that of worshipping God without comprehension of what was being said. Like most people groups, Samoans are very proud of their culture and language. Despite repeated requests, no one was willing to provide an English translation for us. Today, I praise God for what then appeared to be cultural pride and selfishness. Frustrated I went to the mission president and asked be able to visit village churches as the preacher with the plan of taking a student along as translator. The mission president happily agreed and I became an itinerant lay preacher, which forced me to be a better Bible student and also brought us closer to the people of Samoa and to God. God again in his foresight had set me up to gain experience for His future plan for my life.

While at missionary orientation, we attended a class on nutrition in the mission field. We remember adequate protein intake being highlighted and the suggestion that for vegetarians in the mission field it may be necessary to consume some meat to maintain protein intake. Wendy had been raised vegetarian and I had converted to a largely vegetarian diet after marriage. On arrival in Samoa with limited canned vegetarian food being available, we decided that from time to time to eat fresh fish and canned fish. Two events changed this plan. As a boy and teenager, fishing was part of my life. I would prepare the fish by descaling, gutting and de-heading the fish, all of which would be discarded. In Samoa, the fish were gutted and then cooked. On Sabbath the preacher was honoured by being served the largest fish head. With my itinerant preaching schedule, that honour came to me. After the service, the men would all sit around the open Fale (round Samoan house) and the women would serve the men. The women would eat what was left after the men had finished. Each Sabbath I would be presented with a large fish head, often filling most of my plate. That cooked fish head would be looking at me through its now opaque eyes and grinning at me with its sharp teeth. The local people had honoured me with the best they could offer, but this was very unnerving to someone who had grown up on filleted fish. This repeated event coincided with the smell of canned tuna bringing back boyhood memories of feeding my cat canned cat food. Combined, these two events convinced Wendy and I that a low protein vegetarian diet was better than having to eat a fish that was staring at us while we ate it. We returned to a vegetarian lifestyle and then twenty years ago upgraded that to vegan and then to a whole food plant based diet. No regrets and it seems like protein was never an issue as thirty-six years later we are still strong and healthy.

With the transition from boarding school to city based day school, a marked transition came over our students. Many became much less respectful of their teachers causing me considerable stress. By the end of the third year in Samoa, I requested that the South Pacific Division of the Seventh-day Adventist Church reassign me, as the classroom difficulties were taking a toll on my mental well being. God again in His foresight took advantage of this situation, moving us to our next training ground, Fulton College, Fiji.

To live incarnationally, the pride of our culture had to be subdued in order to appreciate the culture of the people we lived among.

Indian Vacation, Boot Camp For Asia

After we married, Wendy and I transferred our membership to the Fremantle Seventh-day Adventist Church in our home state, Western Australia. One Sabbath, a visitor presented to the church the work of the supporting ministry, Asian Aid. At the end of the presentation we were all invited to sponsor a student in India through Asian Aid. Wendy and I were university students living on a government allowance, but despite our very limited financial resources we decided to take on a sponsorship. God was again laying foundations for our future.

At the end of 1986, then two years into our mission experience, we decided to take our vacation in India and visit Asian Aid centres of influence as well as visiting the child we sponsored in Tamil Nadu. Helen Eager, then head of Asian Aid, went out of her way to arrange an itinerary for us that would take us around India and be used by God to continue to lay the foundations for the future work He would have us do in Cambodia. We visited city schools, village schools, Spicer College, attended a Youth Camp and visited orphanages. God was using each of these visits to give us a framework to build His work around many years later in Cambodia. The Indian Adventist people showed this young missionary couple amazing hospitality, which itself would shape the hospitality we would later provide to visitors to our project. Indian people were not new to us, in fact Pastor Stanley who conducted our wedding ceremony was born in India, but through this India tour, Asia had now gained a special place in our hearts.

15

Here I think it is worth mentioning the power of a well prepared children's Sabbath School program to plant seeds in the mind of a child. One Sabbath when I was 11 years old, as a part of the mission story, this beautiful girl entered the Sabbath school classroom dressed in South-east Asian costume. As a child, I instantly fell in love with the girl in the costume. I now realise it was not the girl that I fell in love with, for I had seen her often in Sabbath school, but rather the costume. That costume planted a little bit of Asia in my heart. Another sowing event was in the form of a book on my mother's bookshelf, It was called 'Behind the iron curtain'. While I never read the book, the hand drawn bamboo plant that graced the cover is etched into my mind as a symbol of Asia. These childhood experiences, together with having Asian friends, created a soft spot in my heart for Asia. Back then I had no idea that Asia was God's chosen home for us, but that is still future. First we must move to Fiji.

Beginning a Family

Raising a family in the mission field can be an awesome experience. Wendy and I had decided that there were already enough children in the world and that many of those children did not have a loving home, so the best we could do was to adopt. Our visit to India was in part with that purpose, but it was not to be at that time. Returning to Samoa, we decided to let nature take its course giving God the option of gifting us with children.

We had witnessed missionaries returning to their home country to give birth to their baby where they would have quality medical care and family support around them. Wendy chose the other alternative, give birth in the country where we served, which was Fiji. Caleb was born in Nausouri Provincial Hospital and Shannon born in the small local Korovo district hospital. We had white Fijian boys.

We had discussed and decided that the whole purpose of our boys' education was that they should know God as their Saviour. There were no expectations of them going to university or getting high paying jobs. A second conscious decision was to raise them as local people. To that end, Australia was not referred to as home. Interacting with local kids, eating local food and acquiring the local language were key to this goal. We reasoned that if our children grew up and shared our mission experience with us, the work of God would prosper more than if our children returned to Australia, which in theory at least, was their home country. Caleb chose to go to the local government school where all instruction was in the Khmer language. He home schooled in English as well. Shannon on the other hand, chose home schooling in English until grade 6 at which time he entered formal schooling in the Khmer and English languages at the school we had established.

Hindsight is always helpful. Our boys have grown to be men who work alongside us in mission. For our family, we believe we made God-guided choices with child raising, and are today privileged missionaries as our children work with us, and we can spend time with our grandchildren daily. But now we are getting way ahead in our story.

Fiji, Training Ground Par Excellence

In January, 1988, our family of three moved to Fiji, now three, as Wendy had recently conceived our first son, who would be called Caleb. My assignment was teaching Biology and Chemistry to upper secondary students. In addition, I would lead a team of students in vegetable production much like I did at Kosena College. We moved into an old Mission house that had been moved from the location of the first mission school in Fiji to the Korovo Fulton College Campus. The house was a reminder that many missionaries had gone before us training young people, who by our time of service were Pastors, teachers and church leaders throughout the Pacific islands. The future of God's work depends on local believers finishing the work the foreign missionaries had started. We were grateful to be a part of carrying on the legacy that the missionary pioneers had begun fifty years before at the Korovo Fulton College campus.

Fulton College draws students from the nations all around Fiji, and is a wonderful place to get an exposure to the many unique cultures of the Pacific. It is a place where the uniting factor is a common love for our Lord Jesus Christ. Some of the more memorable events from our first two years in Fiji included the birth of Caleb in the Nausori Provincial Hospital, our whole family of three getting dengue fever one after the other and the subsequent B12 deficiency it induced in Caleb, and the departure of a teacher leaving me with 1.5 teaching loads for the better part of my second year there. At the time, events like these can be traumatic and even life threatening, but when looked back upon can be smiled at, realising that God was in control, even when it seemed He wasn't.

19

Adventist education was my life and any threat to it I saw as a threat to God's Kingdom. A threat arose in 1989, when it was made known that the Union Education Director wanted the Fulton College School Farm, some 200 acres with dairy and beef cattle as well as root crops and vegetable production, to be sold as it was unprofitable. I had been involved in the vegetable production side of the farm. In my thinking this action could not come with the blessing of God, as the farm was more than about making money, it was about the character development of the young people who worked on it. Sale of the farm would create more time for worldly recreation which would result in a weakening of character and spirituality. Impressed by the Holy Spirit, I presented a proposal to the Union president where I would resign from my expatriate teaching position and take on the national position as farm manager. This meant a significant financial change for our family and the loss of many of the benefits that we enjoyed as expatriates, but God's Kingdom was at stake and seeking the good of God's Kingdom together with His righteousness was a core part of what motivated us on a daily basis. My offer was accepted and for the third time in three years we moved house, now being re-located to the school farm.

I threw myself into this new work with all I had to offer, working long days and into the nights, but all the time oblivious to the fact that Wendy and Caleb felt abandoned even though we lived in the same house and saw each other throughout the day. My passion for the Lord's work was creating a rift in my family. This is most definitely a missions problem. I praise God that Wendy bore with me patiently and our marriage survived this difficult time. I also praise God that, while in our two years on the Fulton College farm we did not make it financially viable, steps were taken that in the years to come viability would be achieved. Another significant factor was change of personnel at Union level and with it the change of thinking about the value of the Fulton College farm. The farm was saved, our marriage survived, Shannon our second son was born and God was taking steps to move us strategically to the work He had been training us for.

God Said Adventist Development and Relief Agency And Pastor

The move began with what I would describe as the Holy Spirit speaking to me about God's future plans for our family. Typically when I have heard God, it has always been short and concise, leaving little room for misunderstanding. What I was hearing was that I was to work with the Adventist Development and Relief Agency and be a pastor. The first part made sense as by this time I had gained much experience in multiple areas of tropical agriculture. Becoming a pastor simply seemed an impossibility. I had been ordained as a church elder at the age of 23, and I was serving in the local Fulton College church as Lay Activities leader, but I had no formal theological training and had not attended an Adventist University. I have now learned that If God says it, I should not doubt it. He knows the beginning from the end and where and how the humble submissive disciple can bear the most fruit for the Kingdom of Heaven.

Listening to God is not always easy as our own feelings and thoughts often get in the way. God had said join Adventist Development and Relief Agency so I had applied, but planned to continue serving on the Fulton College farm until an Adventist Development and Relief Agency position came through. This choice came to a sudden change when the new college principal began uncharacteristically throwing his authority around as to how the farm should be run. Without hard feelings I realised that his directions and my experience were not compatible so we made the abrupt choice to return to Australia and wait it out until Adventist Development and Relief Agency called us. The return to Australia in January

1992 came at a time when unemployment was running at a record 11%. Finding a job to support our family of four was apparently going to be difficult. In addition I felt it fair to tell prospective employers that Sabbath work was not an option, and that I could resign at any time as I was awaiting assignment to an overseas project. Neither of these are conducive to finding employment even when jobs are abundant.

With our lives in God's hands, God was free to work out His plan. I visited my lecturers at the state university where I had completed my studies in 1984, asking them if they had any research projects I could work on. A few hours later I left the university with two weeks full-time work and a semester of part-time night teaching at a technical college close to where we had decided to rent a unit. The two week research job transitioned into work that I could have for as long as I was available. Later I realised our abrupt departure from Fiji had a purpose unforeseen at the time. God had work colleagues and College students in Western Australia for me to witness to and there were skills He wanted me to learn in preparation for the next assignment. God even timed it so that the lecturing position would end a couple of weeks before our departure, at that time an unknown date.

I have now learned that If God says it, I should not doubt it. He knows the beginning from the end and where and how the humble submissive disciple can bear the most fruit for the Kingdom of Heaven.

Anywhere! Are You Sure?

Sometime early in April, 1992, Adventist Development and Relief Agency staff contacted us. We were aware of a potential project in Zambia, Africa, which was awaiting funding, but what Adventist Development and Relief Agency offered us came as a surprise. We could choose between Zambia and Cambodia. In Zambia it would involve working in the agriculture fields I was experienced in, Cambodia it would involve working in rice production in which I had no experience. The compound we would live on in Zambia had an Adventist hospital, a useful consideration when raising two small boys. Cambodia was still a war zone after the disastrous Khmer Rouge led civil war, with the national hospital system barely functional.

The biologist in me said Zambia, the mother in Wendy said Zambia, but we gave God the final say, and He chose Cambodia. When God makes His choices known, they often appear to be based on a distinct lack of wisdom to the point of foolishness. Only in hindsight can we realise that God's choices are always best for the Kingdom of Heaven and the individuals concerned.

We had promised God we would go anywhere, and that meant we were going to Cambodia, no matter how dangerous it could potentially be. Already an estimated two million people had been killed in Cambodia after the Khmer Rouge Communists overran Cambodia in 1975. Although this communist regime had lost control of the country in 1979 to the Vietnamese forces, significant pockets of Khmer Rouge soldiers continued to fight to regain Cambodia until 1998, when Pol Pot, the founder of the Khmer Rouge, died.

25

It became apparent that the emotional cost of this assignment could be heavy. Taking two small children into a war zone comes with potential loss. Our three-fold commitment to God now gained a fourth commitment, 'At any cost'. We had read the mission books, they were what God used to get us into the mission field. We knew of the many missionaries who had lost children, their spouse or even their own lives in foreign service with God. We were now ready to make the same commitment if God required it of us. The words of Isaiah come to mind when He said to God,'Here I am, send me.'

This decision did not come without some kickback. Some family members expressed their opinion that it was foolish of us to take our children into an active war zone, but it was to a war zone that we were headed, with Psalm 144:1 and 2 our hope.

Psalm 144:1, 2 (KJV) "Blessed be the Lord my strength, … My goodness, and my fortress; my high tower, and my deliverer; my shield, and He in whom I trust…"

When God makes His choices known, they often appear to be based on a distinct lack of wisdom to the point of foolishness. Only in hindsight can we realise that God's choices are always best for the Kingdom of Heaven and the individuals concerned.

Traveling Back In Time

Our official church call to serve in Cambodia arrived in my parent's mailbox two hours before our scheduled departure for the airport. Sometimes the mission is more urgent than the bureaucracy of the church can keep up with, but when God is in control, all things work toward the best for His Kingdom, or as Paul put it in Romans 8:28 (KJV) "And we know that all things work together for good to them that love God, to them who are the called according to his purpose."

We arrived at the Phnom Penh airport on July 7, 1992. It was stifling hot in the airport and Caleb came down with a fever of 40°C. Not the best welcome to our new assignment. Our family took up residence in a spare room at Murray and Ruth Millar's home in Phnom Penh. Murray was Adventist Development and Relief Agency Cambodia country director. Two days later, I said good bye to my family including a very sick son and headed for Siem Reap not knowing whether I would see Caleb again and missing Shannon's first birthday. God saw Caleb through the illness, and he fully recovered. Through this experience my commitment to the Lord's work was tested.

I settled into a second story room, with shared bathroom down stairs, and no kitchen. Behind my room was the wall to a local Buddhist temple and above my room a flat concrete roof. The first morning as the sun was dawning, I took advantage of the roof as a place to worship God and read the Bible. Around me I could see the smoke of the people's cooking fires rising through the majestic trees that graced the temple grounds. The chant of the monks' morning devotions was clearly audible. As I took in my new environment, I had this distinct feeling that I had travelled back in time at least 100 years. Then as I listened to the creaking sounds of a wooden cart being pulled along by two cows, I had this amazing sensation that after a five month period in Australia feeling somewhat geo-emotionally lost, I was now home. This was most definitely a miraculous event staged by God to confirm that I was where he wanted me to be. Since that early morning event in 1992, Cambodia has been home and its people our people. But still the culture irked me for a number of reasons but that is a story for later.

It did not take long for me to realise why God had chosen Siem Reap as our new home. I thought I had come to Siem Reap to help farmers improve their rice yields, but God had used that as an excuse to move us to a province of Cambodia with a Christian population only barely above zero. We had come to Siem Reap as tentmakers, Adventist Development and Relief Agency work was our income, church planting was our reason for being there.

Today that same building where we first lived in Siem Reap, is a restaurant, somewhat hidden behind taller buildings. Those quaint streets with the old world feeling are busy modern roads with footpaths lined by restaurants, supermarkets and hotels, but the Buddhist temple has changed little and the early morning chants remain the same.

It would be two months before my family would join me. Wendy felt like she was a prisoner in Phnom Penh, finding it difficult to take two small white boys out onto the badly pot-holed streets, in the wet season. In true missionary spirit she moved our family into my one room apartment and did the best she could given the circumstances. It would not be long till life got more bearable as the new Adventist Development and Relief Agency office and house took on liveability.

Do Anything

When we signed up with God to do anything, go anywhere, for any length of time, we had no idea of all the possibilities that promise would entail. In Cambodia, God would reveal what ANYTHING could actually mean. The first of the anythings was architect, building supervisor, carpenter, electrician and plumber. In grade 8 I had completed a subject called 'Technical Drawing', which somehow qualified me as architect. Grades 8-10 woodwork was a subject I enjoyed and qualified me as carpenter. Building supervisor, electrician and plumber were all new qualifications, soon to become essential skills as our ministry opportunities expanded. For me the list continues to grow, having added pastor, international speaker, dentist, etc, etc.

Wendy, who had aspired to work in the area of health sciences, having studied Podiatry soon found herself an English teacher to both children and professional adults. Later Wendy added doctor, midwife, health teacher, home economics teacher, librarian, orphanage director, function organiser, caterer and zoo keeper to mention just a few.

I praise God that He inspired Mrs White to encourage Adventist schools to include vocational training. "Our schools should teach the children all kinds of simple labor." 12LtMs, Lt 104, 1897, par. 20. Today the schools we founded have a strong emphasis on vocational training, having personally experienced its value in promoting mission.

I confess to having a fairly short attention span, to which the do-anything promise has been perfect. God daily arranges for me to work in a multitude of areas, preventing boredom and making everyday fun. God knew my personality, and started skills training early. As a boy I had opportunity to spend afternoons with my grandfather who spent most of his life working in the engine room of submarines and ships, with the later part of his life spent tending flower gardens at an institution for mentally handicapped children. After work he would retreat to his workshop where he would cut and polish gem stones, build furniture and set the stones and shells in resin on the tops of the furniture he built. As a boy I believed my grandfather could do anything, and this belief he imparted to me. The difference between my grandfather and myself is I have Paul's words as my confirmation - "I can do all things through Christ" (Philippians 4:13), and Jesus words promising the Holy Spirit would come as our Teacher (John 14:26). The anything promise has also taught us to be highly flexible in scheduling.

Anything can be something really difficult or something seemingly simple. After helping local people dig a concrete ring well in our garden so that we could have water, I took a bucket with a rope tied to it and tried to get a full bucket of water out of the well. It was a humbling experience to have two neighbour girls aged 5 and 7 come over to teach me the skill required for this apparently simple exercise. Today those two girls, Danee and Dina are both serving the Lord here in Cambodia. A little bit of humility can make a big difference in the Kingdom of Heaven.

I think the most challenging anything God has tossed at me was the design and construction of Butterfly Paradise, which is one of the largest netted butterfly enclosures in the world, but that is a story of faith that comes later in this book.

White Children Work Like A Magnet

When we signed up for Cambodia, the plan was that I would oversee the construction of a house at the agricultural research station about 10 km west of town. By the time we arrived, that plan had been changed and now I was to build an office/house on the second floor of a building that had stood unfinished since the Khmer Rouge had overrun Cambodia almost 30 years before. This building, owned by the agricultural department, was only 200 metres from the central market for the town. Further out of the town on the same road stood one of the town's two high schools. Everyday hundreds of children would pass our new home going to and from school.

Wendy would take our two white-haired, white-skinned boys outside to play, and the boys worked like a magnet on the children passing by. These brown-eyed, brown-skinned, black-haired Khmer children had never seen white children before. They were fascinated, wanting to touch their skin, pinch their cheeks and feel their white hair. It was not long before God began to implement his purpose for the change of our residential location. This constant stream of fascinated children heading to or from school began to ask Wendy to teach them English. The building we were building for house and Adventist Development and Relief Agency office was much larger than needed so we had built a large meeting room at the back of the building. This became the local English classroom, with Wendy as the teacher. Then the staff from the agriculture departments began asking for English lessons. Wendy began teaching three English classes each day Monday to Friday. For Sabbath we offered a bilingual worship program at the same time as the English classes which the eager students came to hoping to learn more English.

The communist government of Cambodia had banned English teaching, wanting to reduce Western influence on the Cambodian people. In 1988 the government began to relax its rules allowing English to again be taught. Many of the townspeople wanted to learn English, creating an evangelistic opportunity to plant the love of God in their hearts. Word spread quickly resulting in more than seventy people daily attending these gospel-flavoured English classes.
From this God started the first Seventh-day Adventist Church in Siem Reap Province.

At Any Cost

Living in Siem Reap town in the early1990's was not for the faint of heart, particularly at night. Virtually every household had an AK47 automatic rifle or a M16 automatic rifle and many households also had grenades. The nights were often punctuated by gunfire and sometimes the sound of a grenade or the anti-aircraft gun mounted on the hill south of town. Theft, particularly of motorbikes, which were hard to come by, was common, and guns were used as a deterrent. Back then few people could drive a car, and cars were mostly limited to the wealthy, the Non-government organisations, and the United Nations peace-keeping troops. The anti-aircraft gun was used for shooting down at Khmer Rouge boats and foot troops that would often use the Tonle Sap lake as a way to approach town at night. From time to time heavy artillery could be heard off in the distance as government troops and Khmer Rouge troops exchanged fire out of town. One night the Khmer Rouge troops launched a missile over the airport into an army compound killing a number of people. Later that day I was working in the fields at the rice research station when I saw an army missile launcher drive past heading north. Shortly after, I heard the hiss of the missiles and the thud at the other end, retaliation for the morning's missiles from the Khmer Rouge. I summed up my situation being not far south from where the missile launcher had unloaded its missiles and concluded in the event of retaliation from the Khmer Rouge my location was not the safest. I went home early that day.

One May morning in 1993, our sleep was disturbed at 4:00 am by a loud explosion. Both Wendy and I sat up in bed in time to see the last of the flash where a rocket

36

propelled grenade had crashed into a Vietnamese enclave about fifty meters from our house. Almost immediately gunfire broke out all over town. The Khmer Rouge had come to town for some fun. We rolled out of bed onto the floor and on our hands and knees headed for the boy's room. Shortly after that we had a makeshift bomb shelter set up in the middle of our house with the wooden dining table lined and covered with mattresses. It was in our little bomb shelter that we remained until the fighting receded into the distance two hours later. Khmer Rouge had stationed themselves under the house next door to us and were shooting at government soldiers across the road. While we had grown accustomed to gunfire, that level of intensity all around us induced fear in our hearts. While God did not stage this event, we believe He took advantage of it to prepare our hearts for a more committed service for Him.

When the fighting had stopped and people were back on the streets, I went out to assess the situation. The Adventist development and Relief Agency's four wheel drive vehicle was untouched by bullets. In fact I could find only one bullet embedded in the wall of our house. The only nearby casualty was a Vietnamese man who had been killed by the initial explosion. It was evident that God had shielded us despite the proximity of the fire fight. At the time all communication with Adventist Development and Relief Agency Cambodia head office in Phnom Penh was by shortwave radio. The order was to evacuate to Phnom Penh as what would happen in the coming days and months was very unclear. Wendy and the boys left on the one and only commercial flight that would leave Siem Reap for the next six months. I stayed behind to give instructions to our Adventist Development and Relief Agency staff and to pray with and encourage the brand new believers whom we had been shepherding to Christ.

The following day I boarded a United Nations C130 military transport plane together with other Non-government workers and headed for Phnom Penh to rejoin my family. Every one on that plane looked to be in deep contemplation of what had just happened. None of us knew whether we would be returning to Siem Reap. All of us had one bag or suitcase. All our personal effects were left behind maybe never to be reclaimed. Our Cambodian friends left behind maybe never to be seen again. We had passports and organisations backing us. We could leave, but the local people could not.

Reunited with my family we headed for Thailand to begin our vacation one week early. While relaxing at a beach on one of Thailand's many islands, Wendy and I reviewed our experience and emotions. The hardest thing for us to grapple with was that we had left our small but growing group of baby Christians behind. We talked to them about an almighty God who loved them, but we ourselves had abandoned them. It was obvious that God had protected us, keeping His promise in Hebrews 13:6, "I will never leave you or forsake you", and that if He could do it once He could do it again. We had not prayed asking if God wanted us to leave, rather we took the first opportunities to board planes and make our way to safety. We had not yet come to the point in our Christian walk where we could say that we were willing to lay down our lives for our Cambodian friends. It was easy to justify leaving, but was it right?

There on the beach, Wendy and I made a promise to God, if this should ever happen again we would not leave unless God Himself told us to. Little did we know that in the coming years we would have similar experiences two more times, and we would have opportunity to test whether we would keep our promise. God had used this experience to bring us to where we were truly ready to promise God that we would do anything, anywhere for any length of time at any cost.

Incarnational Living - The Gift of Poverty

In 1995 our Adventist Development and Relief Agency project in Siem Reap was drawing to a close. We were considering the option to extend our stay and manage the follow-on project. During my morning devotionals I was seeking God and His will for the future. It was then that He spoke to me. Many people ask how I knew it was God. It is hard to explain but I knew it was, besides what I heard was both audacious and crazy all at the same time. I have since learned that God does not usually ask us to do the simple things. He likes to take us out of our comfort zone and into journeys of faith where He can teach us who He really is and how He works with those who will surrender all as they trust Him.

What I heard was this;
1. Work full-time for Me (I knew that meant no salary)
2. Buy land in the countryside (security in the countryside was not good)
3. Use your personal savings to get the project started. (We had about
   US$20,000 saved. No debts or physical assets to speak of)
4. Don't ask anyone for money (Matthew 6:33 came to mind)
5. Live at the same level as the people in the community where you live. (Good bye   mattress and air conditioner.)
6. Start a church in your new community
7. Train lay people to be church planters (I am a biologist and Wendy a podiatrist. We did   not see ourselves as theologians.)

40

God was asking us to take our two small children into the Cambodian countryside where the Khmer Rouge still roamed, live like the local people, buy land and develop the property with our own savings. He wanted us to start another church and train new Adventists to be church planters when we hardly even spoke the language. Not asking anyone for money meant living by faith like George Mueller, one of the missionaries we had read about many years earlier. It was exciting, audacious, dangerous, and crazy from a human perspective.

I broke the news to Wendy. Her response was predictable and sensible, "God did not tell me that." That could have been the end of this story, but we had made a series of promises to God and we had committed to keep those promises. Then there was the waiting time. I was convinced I had heard God even though what I had heard bordered on the absurd. Now God had to convince Wendy. We did not have to wait long. November, 1995 a card arrived from Phnom Penh in the mail. The card was signed John. No return address was given. In the card was a
$60 USD and the words, "I believe in what you are doing. The worker is worth His keep. Matthew 10:10." What God had told me was not public information at that time. For Wendy this was the sign she was looking for. To this day we do not know who John was, for all we know he could have been an angel.

A new journey was about to begin but there were some issues. We had needs, for Wendy it was a proper toilet in the house. At the time, most Khmer village homes had no bathroom or toilet. People bathed at the outside well and toileted behind a bush. For me, I disdained the sound of buzzing mosquitos and wanted screens on the windows of our new house at a time when many Khmer village houses had only three walls and bamboo slats with gaps between them for floors. We had said we would do anything- be careful what you promise God for He is very likely to take you literally. To our knees we went, asking God to help us surrender our needs. Then it happened. One morning we awoke to discover that our needs were no longer needs, what was good enough for the locals was good enough for us. I believe that night as we slept, the Holy Spirit bestowed on us the gift of poverty. Now we could have basically nothing and still enjoy life to the fullest. While Paul never mentions this as a gift, his words to the Philippians seem to indicate he also had been blessed with this gift.

"I have experienced times of need and times of abundance. In any and every circumstance I have learned the secret of contentment, whether I go satisfied or hungry, have plenty or nothing. I am able to do all things through the one who strengthens me." Philippians 4:12, 13 (NET)

We were used to sleeping on an inner spring mattress while the village people slept on a pandanus leaf mat. We ate largely western tasting food, while the village people ate rice two or three times a day with a soup or fish. We drove an Adventist Development and Relief Agency four wheel drive vehicle, the village people mostly rode bicycles. We lived in a brick house with glass windows, the village people mostly lived in houses with thatched walls made of palm leaves with a dried grass roof. The contrasts were great, but by the grace of God we would adapt to enjoy our new God given lifestyle. In preparation, the mattress was replaced with a pandanus mat on the carpet of the Adventist Development and

Relief Agency house. Food changed till rice was the staple. Life was being simplified, to the point it became a game of giving up something cherished for something better, simplicity.

The date for the last Adventist Development and Relief Agency pay cheque approached, December 31, 1995. Our life savings would run out not long into our new project. Would God be good with His promise in Matthew 6:33, "Seek you first the Kingdom of God and His righteousness and all these other things will be added to you"?
I like to expand that verse as I had been seeking the Kingdom of God, but now I would be seeking the good of the Kingdom of God and Kingdom expansion.

As I sit writing this, it is almost December 31, 2023. Twenty-eight years have elapsed since the last monthly pay cheque. God has kept His promise above and beyond our imagination, all glory to Him. But again we are skipping key events in the journey that is ongoing.

I have since learned that God does not usually ask us to do the simple things. He likes to take us out of our comfort zone and into journeys of faith where He can teach us who He really is and how He works with those who will surrender all as they trust Him.

Life was being simplified, to the point it became a game of giving up something cherished for something better, simplicity.

Independent, and One

When Jesus left His disciples to return to heaven, He apparently left no one in charge. What
He told the disciples was to wait for the outpouring of the Holy Spirit and then to take the gospel to the world. The Holy Spirit was sent to replace Jesus as leader. The disciples were to work together with the Holy Spirit, taking their individual directions from the Holy Spirit while working harmoniously with each other to advance the kingdom of God.

When God called us to start SALT Ministries, a ministry that supports the spiritual mission of the Seventh-day Adventist Church but is an independent supporting ministry not controlled by or legally affiliated with the Church, He spoke directly to me, not to the leaders of the church. Thankfully, Pastor Daniel Walter, then president of the Cambodia Adventist Mission, was very supportive of the directions that the Holy Spirit had given, encouraging our family to move forward with God's plans. He understood that Christ is the head of the church and the members are the body, each with a different calling but all with a common purpose- the advancement of the Kingdom of Heaven here on earth. Pastor Walter also understood that God's calling is more important than the worldly qualifications we have to fulfil that calling. Having been called to train church planters, I questioned Pastor Walter about my suitability to God's calling having never received formal theological training. I believe his response was Spirit inspired for it gave me freedom to be led by the Spirit. He responded by saying that for the work God had called us to do, it was probably better that I had not received theological training. I understood that to mean that I had not been institutionally programmed, therefore I was free to be led by the Spirit in the way that God wanted it done in this situation.

From our perspective, we were called to compliment what the Cambodia Adventist Mission were doing, providing services that they were either not called to provide or not free to provide due to finance, human resources or policy. God discerned the need and chose to work through independent agents to fill that need, but always with the intent that the ministry of the Cambodian Adventist Mission and SALT Ministries should be one. The existence of the Cambodian Adventist Mission was essential to the success of the ministry God had called our family to, and at the same time the fruit of SALT Ministries would ultimately enhance the ability of the Cambodia Adventist Mission to achieve it's goal of evangelising Cambodia. As time passed God sent other supporting ministries to further complement the work done in Cambodia, with the Cambodian Adventist Mission welcoming them as it had welcomed us. Cambodia is an excellent example of how much more can be achieved for the work of God when the organised church welcomes and works harmoniously together with supporting ministries.

In Cambodia several large schools are funded and operated by supporting ministries, but counted as Cambodia Mission schools. Others are run by the Mission but supported financially by supporting ministries. This level of cooperation has resulted in a significant number of children coming from Adventist homes, attending Adventist schools in a country where government schooling is compulsory on Sabbath and students are encouraged to pay homage to idols.

Each of these Adventist schools operate with different focus on education, therefore providing future workers for the church with a wide range of experience and a more diverse skill set.

While policy is essential to the long term stable existence of the work of God in any country, SALT Ministries unencumbered by policy has been able to work agilely and adaptively in a way the organised church can not. As a faith based ministry, we are not obliged to work within budgets, in fact we have not had budgets, but instead we are free to move forward in faith, trusting God to provide the means as needed to make each project a success. This is not to say the organised church is wrong because they have policy and work within preset budgets, but rather that God in a complimentary way uses both models to finish His work.

Cambodia is an excellent example of how much more can be achieved for the work of God when the organised church welcomes and works harmoniously together with supporting ministries.

The Joy Of Imminent Death

Our pre-missionary diet of mission story books taught us something about mission that many would rather not think about, mission work can be dangerous and sometimes deadly. It was not difficult to promise God we would go anywhere, do anything for any length of time, but the additional promise at any cost did not come so easily. With that promise now behind us, opportunities for Satan to test the sincerity of that promise would most certainly arise. When we began our ministry, security even short distances outside of the town of Siem Reap was often questionable. In June, 1996 we moved to the ministry land five kilometres out of Siem Reap town. The local authorities were not altogether comfortable with us being somewhat isolated out on our ministry land, as security, particularly at night, could not be guaranteed.

By March 1997, it appeared that the authorities fears were unfounded, until one night, while cooking pineapple jam. Wendy's kitchen was a small clay cooking stove on the ground under a lean-to that we had added to our house. The palm leaf and bamboo door was still open when 9 pm came around. The boys were asleep under a mosquito net in the house and our small 12 V light provided just enough light through the open doorway for us to see immediately in front of our simple bamboo and thatch home. Wendy and I were having a conversation about what it would take to reach the people in our local community with the gospel. We had been there 8 months and had made very few inroads for the gospel. In an apparently prophetic utterance, Wendy spoke about the importance of us experiencing what our neighbours experienced. (Being robbed at gunpoint at night was one of those experiences that all of our neighbours feared, even though most of them had at least one AK 47 automatic rifle in their home.) No more than 30 seconds elapsed after this sentence when the parrots in the cage attached to our house began to flutter around in the dark. I stepped out of the door way of our house and shone a flash-light around to look for the cause of the disturbance, expecting to see a dog passing by. I was caught by surprise when my flashlight illuminated three AK 47 automatic rifles pointed at me. Not wishing our three male visitors to enter, I backed back into the elevated doorway of our house.

Money was demanded, to which Wendy responded by passing a small roll of money to them through the doorway. The small bundle of Khmer riel, was valued at just over US$3 and was obviously inadequate as it was thrown back through the doorway into the house. One of our visitors stepped forward, raising his gun so that the end of the gun barrel was only centimetres below my chin. As I looked down the barrel, I saw two concerning things, firstly a finger was on the trigger and secondly the face of our visitor was quite obviously not happy. The potential cost of this incident flashed across my mind with the realisation that my head could very likely explode from the impact of a bullet passing through it. Death stared me in the face. At such times like this, it is amazing how fast the brain can process and analyse information, and then pose questions that needed an immediate answer. The question that my brain posed was , "do you really believe you are saved by the blood of Jesus?"

Of course I believed I was saved by the blood of Jesus, that's why I was a missionary. But some-how the question was calling for not just a flippant answer but an answer that came from the heart. An answer that would bring either peace or fear. As I stared down that gun barrel, I silently answered that question with, "Yes, it is ok if I die right now. I am saved by the blood of Jesus and I will see Jesus when He returns to take the righteous home." Immediately I felt a joyful warmth emanating from my heart. It is hard to describe or explain but I knew at that moment that the presence of God was with me. Fear was banished and in its place was peace that felt euphorically awesome. As I was enjoying the moment, a rapid movement from the assumed leader of the three, disturbed my vision. He stepped forward and shoved his friend so hard that his friend fell to the ground dropping his gun. It all happened so fast that to this day I assume it was the leader, but maybe it was an angel. If our visitor was unhappy before, now he was quite obviously angry. As he rose to his feet he took hold of the gun barrel and swung with all his might. The steel folding handle of the gun slammed into the side of my lower left leg with such force I was surprised that my bones had not broken. I think at that moment the euphoria from the presence of God shielded me from pain. I spoke calmly telling our visitors that I would get them money. As I stepped out of the doorway, Wendy bravely replaced me blocking their entrance to the house. I calmly walked without a limp across to the filing cabinet in which I had two bundles of money. One bundle was comprised of ten one hundred dollar notes and the other was Khmer riel valued at about US$18. I believe the Holy Spirit inspired me to reason that our visitors did not know how much money we had in the house that night so if I gave them the Khmer money they would leave, which is exactly what happened.

With our three visitors departing into the darkness, we dropped to our knees and gave thanks to God for His protection and then I went to the house about 50 meters from ours to inform our assistant, Prak Heng, what had happened. The local police were called who then called a contingent of police from the town to join them. The police also armed with AK 47 riffles showed no desire to venture into the darkness to look for our assailants, and eventually left the property around midnight. Grateful for their care and equally grateful to be finally able to get some sleep, we climbed under our mosquito net and slept peacefully in the arms of God.

Even without the internet, rumours travel quickly and the next day we were at the centre of one of those rumours both in our village and in the town. The story of our three visitors and their escapades was being told. The rumour had various flavours including that I had been shot, and I had a broken leg, neither being true but making for good gossip. Behind the scenes God was silently working with the rumours to advance His Kingdom in Cambodia. We were foreigners with two small boys, living like peasants in a rural Cambodian community. We had not yet been assimilated into our community, but that was about to change. Having experienced this harrowing event it was assumed by most that we would pack up our things and move back to the safety of our home country Australia. When this assumption proved to be wrong and we continued to live in our isolated thatched house and continue with life as normal, the local people began seeing us as part of their community and heart doors began to open to the gospel. When God's people are faithful no matter what, God expertly takes Satan's best planned attacks and turns them to His own advantage. God spared no cost for our salvation and we now have the privilege of working in partnership with God at any cost.

When God's people are faithful no matter what, God expertly takes Satan's best planned attacks and turns them to His own advantage. God spared no cost for our salvation and we now have the privilege of working in partnership with God at any cost.

If God Said It, He Meant It

When God makes a promise, He will always keep His promise if we keep ours. In calling us to supporting ministry, God had clearly told me to use all our own funds to get started and that He would provide the rest as needed. We began our ministry on January 1, 1996. Fast forward to June 1997.

Elder Mike Ryan, at that time in charge of Global Mission at the General Conference, had visited Siem Reap a couple of times and was aware of the calling God had given us to train church planters (also known as Global Mission Pioneers). Under the inspiration of the Holy Spirit, Elder Ryan brought businessman Denzil McNeilus to meet us and hear the vision God had placed on our heart. This was to be a pivotal God engineered meeting for our ministry and the growth of the church in Cambodia. I rode my bicycle the 5 km into town for the initial meeting with Denzil and Elder Ryan. The first lesson Denzil taught me was that bicycles are useful but too slow to finish taking the gospel to all the world. I was grateful to hear this as I had been praying for funds to buy a second hand motorcycle. Denzil had a car in mind, which I argued against as we were called to live incarnationally and in 1997, no one in our immediate villages owned a car. We settled on a new off-road motorcycle. Lesson learned, don't underestimate what God would like to give. I would have been happy with a second-hand motorbike but God had a new one in mind. I have since learned to tell God about the need and let Him decide on the solution. The next lesson Denzil taught me was that while living by faith in God's provision is excellent, it is wise to have some idea of what God's

53

provision is going to cost. When asked how much money did we need to train church planters, and initiate, and fund 10 church plants over a three year period, my answer was "I do not know, God will provide". To that Denzil responded that he had not travelled half way around the world only to be told that I did not know how much money was needed to get training and church planting going. Denzil kindly spent time with me helping me put together a budget which he generously funded.

About a year later, Denzil returned to Cambodia and we discussed how the plan for training and church planting was going. It was not going well as we had not yet been able to recruit people to train. Now Denzil would teach me a third lesson about finishing God's work in this generation. Money given for God's work is money that is to be spent, not left sitting in a bank earning interest. He kindly gave me one more year to spend the money or return it so it could be put to work saving souls somewhere else. It took nearly six months more to recruit our first cohort for church planter training, but in God's timing it happened and today there are church groups across Siem Reap province worshipping as a result of that visit in 1997.

Learning to trust God has been a journey. Most of us would say we trust God, but when the going gets tough, the big question is how far does that trust extend. Let me give you a current example. Our ministry does not make its needs known but simply trusts God to provide our needs. Each month we need about US$16,000 to pay wages, feed more than 120 children, pay the power bill, etc, etc. This month we received just over USD$2000 in donations at the beginning of the month. We have zero financial reserves. The way I see it is that we have four choices: 1. Close down our ministry, 2. Borrow money, 3. Make our urgent needs known, or 4. Trust God to keep His promise. God has made us the promise that if we seek first His Kingdom and His righteousness all these other things will be added to us. For God, failing to keep His promise is not an option. But His promise is conditional, and trust is built into it. We have operated at this level of trust for 28 years now, and God has never failed us. So in our current financial situation, should we be concerned? If it was just our family it would be one thing, but when we have orphans and Adventist dorm students and staff depending on us, many would say we need to act responsibly and do something. For us the responsible action is to trust God, and wait on Him to do something.

When the Israelites spent forty years in the wilderness, they were continually dependent on God for their needs. He provided six days each week, ensuring they had enough for seven. We have nicknamed wilderness living as 'Manna Months'. The day the Israelites entered the land of Canaan they had plenty and the manna stopped. Months when there is money in the bank are nicknamed Canaan months. It is always nice to have a safety margin (Canaan month), but it is exciting to see God work miracles daily (Manna month). When the 'Time of Trouble" arrives, and God's people cannot buy or sell, all of His people will need to trust Him absolutely. Fear of God failing to keep His promise will likely lead some to capitulate to breaking the Sabbath, excusing themselves with the thought that God would not want their families to suffer hunger. We praise God that our twenty-eight years of experience confirms that God is more than able to fulfil His promises if we don't hinder Him with our doubt.

Elijah is a good example to us. God used ravens to bring him food while he was at the brook Cherith. When he was with the widow and her son, the flour and oil never ran out. And then when Elijah was fleeing to the mountain of God, God fed him twice and the food gave him strength to travel for forty days and nights. I am still learning to tell God about the problem, and then in childlike simplicity believe that He already has the best solution.

Evacuate or Stay?

The Khmer Rouge attack on Siem Reap town in 1993, led Wendy and I to make the decision that should something like that ever happen again we would not leave unless God Himself told us to. July 1997 found our family in Phnom Penh to purchase a motorcycle and computer. The motorcycle was to be ready on Thursday afternoon and we would transport it by boat back to Siem Reap on Friday. Tickets had already been purchased when I went to pick up the motorbike from the Yamaha dealer. On arrival I discovered the motorcycle would not be fully assembled until the following day. This did not fit my itinerary. I was about to raise my voice in protest when the silent voice of the Holy Spirit spoke to me telling me to let it go and come back tomorrow. That meant losing money on the boat tickets and having to stay through to Sunday as we would not travel during the Sabbath. Trusting the Holy Spirit to know what was right, I forced a smile and told the salesman I would be back tomorrow. Sabbath morning, July 5, 1997, found us in an English Sabbath school at the Adventist Development and Relief Agency office in Phnom Penh. Toward the end of the Sabbath school class, one of the participants received a phone call from a friend high up in government advising her to take shelter at her home as a coup d'état was about to take place. Sabbath school ended abruptly and everyone returned to their dwellings. Several hours passed before the gunfire started. It was not long before people were fleeing the fighting passing the Cambodia Adventist Mission head quarters. Not so long later we saw the same people returning, as the direction in which they were fleeing was also experiencing heavy fighting. From the mission compound we could hear tanks manoeuvring in the nearby streets and the loud bangs as they fired their shells. Fighting went on for two days before moving slowly away across country to the north-west.

During this experience I found reason to praise God for the 1993 Khmer Rouge attack in Siem Reap. There I had learned to trust my family and my life into God's hands. This time we feared
God rather than being in fear of death and this gave us opportunity to encourage the mission staff and church members who had taken shelter at the Mission compound.

With the shelling over we ventured out to see the damage. On the main road to the airport a tank was badly damaged. Shops, warehouses and car sales yards were looted. But we were all safe.

It was not long before the South-East Asian Union president was on the phone to the mission officers instructing that all foreigners were to evacuate at the first possible opportunity. He also spoke with me asking me to evacuate our family. I thanked him for his concern, then said that as volunteers working independent of the Cambodia Adventist Mission, we chose to stay. His next words surprised me. He said if that was our decision could we stay in Phnom Penh and help to run the mission until the mission officers returned.

Instead of taking a boat to Siem Reap on the Sunday as planned, we stayed in Phnom Penh for nearly two months, standing in for the mission president. What a privilege and blessing that was to be able to work with the mission staff and church members in Phnom Penh. I now believe that the Holy Spirit was behind the delay in the preparation of the motorcycle. God had a work for us to do in Phnom Penh that we would never have imagined. We learned that God's agenda is often very different from our own. Again we could see how God had been setting everything up so that at the right time we would be where He wanted us. How often we complain to God when things don't go according to our plans. Instead of complaining maybe we should be apologising to God for not including Him in our planning and not seeking to know His agenda for our lives.

Even after all these years I am still finding it difficult to go to God with my plans and then say, nevertheless, whatever is Your will I want to be in the centre of it. I believe Jesus went to God early each day to ask God what is on the schedule for the day. How much easier it would be for God, and ourselves, if we were to be like Jesus.

We learned that God's agenda is often very different from our own.... How often we complain to God when things don't go according to our plans. Instead of complaining maybe we should be apologising to God for not including Him in our planning and not seeking to know His agenda for our lives.

Do Anything. Doctor? MidWife?

After purchasing land for developing the training centre, a road needed to be constructed to access the property and a fence needed to be erected around the land. These two projects gave us opportunity to employ local village people and begin to get to know them. It was not long before these neighbours began asking Wendy if she could help them with their medical problems. This was the birth of our ministry's medical work. Wendy had some medical training acquired while gaining her diploma in podiatry. Added to this she had experience as school nurse both in Samoa and Fiji. Now God was ready to take Wendy to another level by bringing people to her with all kinds of medical problems.

The medical work began on the small porch in front of our new two story wooden house, but God had bigger plans. Two, one thousand dollar donations enabled us to build a spacious single story wooden facility to function as outpatient clinic, hospital and temporary training centre. This building had a clinic room, two small rooms for in-patients, small kitchen and bathroom and a larger open waiting room. Simple but adequate.

Patients began to line up. Each patient would be interviewed, examined, counselled, prayed with and given medication as appropriate. The book, 'Where there is no Doctor' was our go-to for understanding the nature of the disease and the treatment. Wendy was home schooling Caleb and Shannon, and taking care of inpatients and up to 30 outpatients a day. Often, I would have to fill for her as doctor, falling back on my biology training and knowledge gleaned from our many years of mission work.

Many times our knowledge of the cause of illness was Holy Spirit given. One day a boy of 10 years, was brought to us with severe abdominal pain. Appendicitis was an option, but while silently praying I heard the Holy Spirit say 'worms, send him to the hospital'. For worms we would normally give medication and send the patient home, but this time we instructed the parents to take their child straight to the hospital. Later that day the doctors operated and removed a large ball of worms that were obstructing the child's intestines. We had no ultra sound equipment but the eye of the Holy Spirit sees all things.

Most births in the village were managed by a traditional birth attendant, who had no formal training but lots of experience. One of the women who had been joining our Sabbath programs invited us to be present at the delivery of her child. She had recently kicked her drunken husband out and sadly had no desire to be caring for another child. When we arrived we found her in labor attended by the traditional birth attendant and two helpers. The labour progressed slowly and the birth attendant and helpers decided to hasten the process by applying significant pressure on the woman's abdomen to help push the baby out. This procedure was successful and the baby was delivered but in a spastic state, jerking continually. We believe that the excessive pressure may have damaged the baby's spinal cord due to being a face presentation. The baby stopped breathing about twenty minutes after delivery. The mother seemed relieved that the child was dead, and asked relatives to take the body and bury it. Babies and small children who die are buried in a shallow grave with no ceremony. I asked if I could have the honour of burying the baby and my request was granted. I brought the lifeless body of the little girl back to our graveyard, gave her the name Maranatha, and buried her asking God to count her as my daughter and put her in my arms at the second coming. As Wendy and I reflected on the events of the day, Wendy decided that with the help of the Holy Spirit, she could help women deliver much safer than what we had just witnessed. That was the beginning of a new skill, midwifery. The book, 'A Book for Midwives' (Hesperian Foundation), became her delivery companion and she went on to deliver more than 60 babies until the health system was able to provide safe midwifery services.

How often have we turned down God-given opportunities with the excuse that we are not qualified. If we are tempted to say no, because we consider ourselves unqualified, remember Jesus dispatched the Holy Spirit to ensure we have a coach. God wants to up-skill us to finish taking the gospel to all the world. Our experience has shown me that God gets a thrill out of training us in the place He has chosen for us to work.

Showered with Amniotic Fluid

Not all baby deliveries go to plan and this story is most definitely one I will not forget. We were well into our first Church Planter training program when one of our married students reached full term. She was a very short young lady and this was her second delivery (her first being stillborn), both of these points are potentially problematic. It was already nighttime when labor started coming on strong. She chose to have Wendy deliver her baby in the upstairs of our home. Labor was moving along slowly and at about 10 pm the expectant mother decided she would like to take a warm bucket shower on our front verandah. This we could accommodate but beneath the veranda I had many 60 kg sacks of our recently harvested unmilled rice which I first had to move to another location. The expectant mother was standing on the verandah above me when warm water poured directly on my head. I shouted with an annoyed voice, that she was not to take a shower until I had finished moving the sacks of rice. Her attendants replied with the news that her water had just broke. The water that had soaked my head and upper body was not water but rather amniotic fluid, definitely a very unique event that could only happen in the mission field. The lady showered and continued waiting on the arrival of her baby. I went out to our well and washed the amniotic fluid off, putting plenty of shampoo on my hair. Another hour or so ticked by and still no progress. At around midnight, the young lady decided she would go for a walk outside together with her attendants who were carrying a single kerosene lamp made out of a condensed milk can. We were all half asleep upstairs, when I heard from outside a cry that the baby was coming, I sprang to my feet and down the steep steps then out the front door. There in the dim light of the lamp, I saw the mother lying on the cement porch and the baby's head crowning. I ran around the mother and dived my open hand and arm landing between the mother's legs as the baby made its dramatic entry into the world. To this day I can only say the Holy Spirit inspired me to make the dive and catch the child. My delivery count still stands at one and I have no desire to change that; one was memorable enough. The mission field is a place of adventure where unique memorable stories are made for the retelling, and simple acts of kindness make an eternal difference.

Honey, We Have a Daughter

In the late 1990's HIV was rampant in Cambodia because married men would supplement their sexual activity with visits to prostitutes, and then bring the virus home as a gift for their wives and often their unborn child. Anti-retroviral drugs were not yet available and stigma about the viral disease was strong. Women who contracted the disease from their husbands usually outlived their husbands leaving only the children to care for them in their dying days. Often extended family were too afraid to be closely involved, fearing they would contract the disease as well.

Our bush hospital became a hospice to ladies dying of AIDS. One of these ladies had been watching her neighbours as they transitioned from being Buddhist to being Christian. She recognised her end was near and made the decision to die Christian in a Christian place and came to us for care. She left her three sons to care for the home, animals and farm and brought her seven year old daughter to help take care of her. While we could do nothing to cure her, we could show her love and do our best to make her as comfortable as possible while she waited her tragic end. Like many of those who were beyond medical cure, she gave her life to Christ before the end came, dying with the hope of resurrection at the second coming of Jesus. I had spent very little time with her seven year old daughter Ly (said Lie), but when Ly's mother passed to her rest, I had the sad responsibility of explaining what had happened. I scooped Ly up in my arms and sat on a chair. As the realisation set in that she was now an orphan, she buried her face in my chest and cried for about half an hour. Then it was decision time, what next? We had no orphanage at the time, but this tragic event would be instrumental in us later opening an orphanage for children just like Ly. I knew the options. Go live with her older unmarried brothers who would now have to fend for themselves, go live with her aunty who already had three girls, or come live with our family. The third option I had not discussed with Wendy. Ly thought through her options and indicated she would come live with us. Wendy got quite a surprise when I came home with a seven year old girl and announced that we have a daughter. From that day to this, Ly has been a part of our family. Today Ly and her husband Rachou, also orphaned because of AIDS, have two school aged boys who call us grandma and grandpa.

In this world there are so many orphaned and vulnerable children. If these children were to experience the love of Christ in Christian homes, there is a high probability that they would give their lives to Jesus and prepare for His soon return. In talking to the saved at the second coming, Jesus will say, "you invited me in when I was a stranger". They will answer, "when did we see you a stranger and invite you in." Jesus will reply, "just as you did it for one of the least of these brothers or sisters of mine, you did it for me" Matthew 25:34-40.

In this world there are so many orphaned and vulnerable children. If these children were to experience the love of Christ in Christian homes, there is a high probability that they would give their lives to Jesus and prepare for His soon return.

Make Disciples

Jesus directed the attention of His disciples to nearby wheat fields, telling the disciples the fields are ripe for harvest but the harvesters are few. He followed this up by telling the disciples to pray to the Father for more harvesters Matthew 9:37, 38.

Having personally harvested our own rice using a short sharp sickle, I can tell you it is hot, back-breaking work that requires technique, endurance and persistence. Jesus recognised that harvesting this world for the Kingdom of Heaven was a greater task than twelve disciples could handle, therefore He also told them to make disciples and teach them everything He had taught them: technique, endurance and persistence. Today the field of this world continues to be ripe and the harvesters are still few. This was especially true in 1993, when Cambodia was just reopening to the Three Angels' Messages (Revelation 14:6-12). As Adventist Christians returned from the refugee camps in Thailand and began sharing their faith with their Buddhist neighbours, some of these neighbours accepted Jesus as their Saviour. The problem was, and still is, that from Buddhism to true Christianity is like travelling from the earth to the moon; it is a difficult and long journey. God saw the need to jump start this process and for reasons only known to Him, chose our family to do it from here in Siem Reap.
The only qualifications we could claim for this calling were that we are baptised Adventists, I was ordained as an elder in Samoa, and at the time we were tent-making (working for Adventist Development and Relief Agency and planting a church in our free time). To that short list we could add one more qualification, probably the most

important- we were willing to do what ever God asked even if it was outside our expertise and comfort zone.

We chose to recruit students through the network of pastors, empowering the pastors to choose who should come to the training. This proved problematic to begin with as the pastors knew me as an agriculturalist working for Adventist Development and Relief Agency, not a trainer of future pastors. Failing to recruit from around the country we turned to people in our own province and the neighbouring province of Oddar Meanchey, places where we were known as Christian leaders more than Adventist development and Relief Agency workers. We enrolled 20 people in our first training, then two weeks in, added another family who had just decided to believe in Jesus. Four months later we sent these trainees out as families or in twos when they were singles. We let the trainees prayerfully choose their fields of labor, and then provided spiritual, logistical and financial support to help them plant a church. When word reached the pastors in other provinces that Siem Reap was experiencing church growth as a result of our training program, many came on board, sending their new disciples to join our training programs. Over a period of 10 years we held 12 training programs training about four hundred people. We did not do all of the training by ourselves. Some Union departmental directors assisted as did Cambodia Adventist Mission departmental directors.

As always, God's timing is perfect. In 1999, while our second batch of students was training, global mission money filtered its way down through the system to the Cambodia Adventist Mission. On graduation of these students, the Mission was financed and organised to send them out around the country to begin planting new churches in unentered provinces. The Seventh-day Adventist church entered a period of rapid church growth country-wide. This was not by the wisdom of men but because God took time to implement His plan in Cambodia, and because lay people like ourselves, and the Cambodia Adventist Mission supported by the world church, worked as one toward finishing God's work.

Ten years on, the country of Cambodia was changing from one of the poorest countries in the world to having a fast growing economy. Satan strategically used the influx of money to distract attention away from spiritual things to material things and church growth slowed and went backwards. By 2008, the Pastors could no longer supply us with the lay students needed to continue the four month training program. God was already ahead of Satan having another timely strategy in mind, the education of His children in Adventist schools.

The Unicorn in the Room

A unicorn is a mythical, horse-like animal which stands out as being different because of its large single horn in the centre of its forehead. In a herd of horses a unicorn will immediately be noticed as being different. This is true also with missionaries working with cultural groups different from their own. The most immediate differences are skin colour, hair colour/type/style, eye colour and body height, to this we can also add dress type if the people the missionary is working with have their own cultural style of dress. Language and accent also add to the unicorn effect, as do religion, diet, and social connectedness.

A missionary can take steps to shorten the horn, like learning the language, following cultural norms for dress, etc, but the cross cultural missionary will always be a unicorn in the culture they are working with.

Ironically, for a time at least, attempts to shorten the horn, like dressing like the people, speaking their language and living like them may actually make the cross cultural missionary stand out even more as they do not fit the ethnic stereotype the local people are expecting in their foreigner.

In 1996 when our family moved out into the country side to live incarnationally with the Khmer village people, we became an ethnic spectacle. The local people understood that caucasian people live in big houses, wear fancy clothes and drive nice cars. Our family broke this stereotype by living in a small house made of palm leaves, bamboo, grass and wooden poles just like their own houses. We slept on a mat on the floor under a mosquito net, dressed like them, rode bicycles like them, grew rice like them, and bathed at an outside cement ring well like them. Wendy cooked Khmer food on a small clay cooking stove like them and we ate rice three times a day like them. This incarnational lifestyle that God had called us to was a novelty to our neighbours. Visiting our home and watching us foreigners became a popular pastime in our community. We had visited ethnic groups in other countries who stood out as being different and therefore were on the tourist circuit of things to see. Now we had become like those people and we were on the local tourist circuit. We gained an understanding of how it feels to be a spectacle, which has profoundly impacted the way we view ethnic differences. Overtime, as we interacted and loved the people, we became accepted and the differences diminished, but no matter how good our local accent is, how similar our food is, or how familiar the architectural style of our home, we are still unicorns, albeit with a shorter horn.

The differences in religion significantly contribute to the unicorn effect. The big social events here in Cambodia revolve around religious understanding and practice, which are a syncretistic mixture of animism, ancestral worship, Hinduism and Buddhism. While there are many things that we can adopt from the culture of the local people, even from the forms they use in the practice of their religion, contextualisation must have its limits or the distinctiveness of the gospel will be lost. These differences make us stand out and may be barriers in themselves, but they can also be used to the advantage of the Kingdom of Heaven. An example is music. Khmer people like singing, but song does not feature in their religious practices. Christian songs in the local language and using local tunes sung in the homes of villagers tend to draw people in to listen which provides opportunities to share God.

Understanding the worldview of a people group is near impossible until it can be understood in the language of that people group. Without that understanding many things that feature in the daily lives of that people group may remain obscure or hidden. Because of stereotypes, local people may assume that the foreigner would not understand their lives and therefore they would not share certain aspects of life. This is particularly true regarding the world of the supernatural. Only when we spoke enough Khmer language to sit in people's homes and converse with them about everyday events did we understand the significant role the spirit world played in their daily lives. When they realised that we understood and did not ridicule their experience, opportunities began to open up for power encounters which otherwise would never have happened. With power encounters came the realisation that the God of the Christians is more powerful than the spirit world that dominates their lives, and this realisation often led to change in spiritual allegiance and the peace of God replacing the fear of reprisal from the spirits.

The missionaries' diet may also create the unicorn effect. Wendy and I live on a whole food plant based diet, while most of our Khmer brothers and sisters in Christ choose to live on a clean meat diet. When they eat at functions we organise, they are happy to eat vegetarian food, but in their own gatherings meat will be significantly featured. When we join their gatherings, we are quite obviously the unicorns in the group, and by not being present we are still the unicorns. We could compromise our lifestyle when eating with them, but then we would fail to model the importance of a heaven designed diet for health and spirituality. The probability of sickness is also high as our immune systems are not used to having to deal with the bacterial contamination that comes with eating meat that has not been refrigerated.

We have learned to live with the fact that we will always be unicorns to a greater or lesser degree, even in Australian culture. Having lived in other cultures for 38 years out of our sixty, the culture we grew up in has changed in our absence and we have changed. Visiting Australia is almost as foreign to us as going to a European country that we have not previously visited. Our lifestyle of incarnational living in Christ is a world apart from the life we would be living had we chosen to remain in Australia. We can visit but we no longer fit. For our children who grew up in Cambodia, the cultural differences between them and Australians are greater than the cultural differences between them and Cambodians. Mission has changed us. We now identify best as citizens of the Heavenly Kingdom. Today we are unicorns, but soon with the second coming of Jesus we will no longer stand out as being different. In heaven we will rejoice in our differences while all being one in Christ.

Satan Calls Down Fire

Dealing with the demonic was not new to me, but the story I tell here takes it to a whole new level. But first a little background. As a teenager I would pass through the city centre of Perth in Western Australia on my way home from school. As a nature enthusiast I visited book shops looking for books on animals and plants. On one occasion I saw a new bookshop spilling out on to the street so I entered and headed toward the back taking no notice of what kind of books were for sale. Toward the back of the shop I began to feel nauseous and dizzy. This feeling of un-wellness had come in a matter of seconds. Feeling something was not right I stopped and looked at the books and realised I was in a bookshop that sold books on witchcraft. Immediately I exited the store and the nausea and dizziness left. I had stepped on Satan's ground and he had made it clear as a child of God, I was not welcome. Years later while working at Kosena College, in Western Samoa, one of our students had a habit of becoming zombie-like on the sports field when something had upset him. He demonstrated super strength, did not communicate and was quite rigid in his movements. This behaviour became more and more frequent often happening on Friday nights causing disruption to the Sabbath. The principal Vic Bonetti, and myself, concluded this was demonic and had a biblical style deliverance session for the young man. The problem ceased. Then in 1989 at Fulton College, Fiji, I had a small altercation with a Solomon Island student during an evening study period. While he had his hands around my throat and my head pressed down on a desk I looked into his eyes and was surprised to see what appeared to be rivulets of fire running through his eyes. Later some of the girls from the dorm told me they had seen this young man walk through the walls of the girls dormitory holding some kind of fetish in one of his hands.

Fast forward to 1998, and a lady arrives at Wendy's clinic with more than 30 small burn marks on her torso. After Wendy had questioned and examined her, she called me to take care of this patient as the problem appeared spiritual in origin. After questioning the lady, I came to the same conclusion. She previously had a dreadlock that was shaped like a man. She had it cut off by Buddhist monks who advised her to take care of the dreadlock. She had a variety of medical type ailments including a marble sized lump in her back that could move up and down. The burns were an attempt by a Cambodian traditional healer (known as a Kru Khmer, which translates Khmer teacher) to drive out evil spirits using a burning incense stick. He was unsuccessful, so the lady decided to try out the Christian doctor to see if she could help. Having heard her story, I concluded the Kru Khmer was right about evil spirits, but wrong about how to set the lady free. I asked the lady to have her husband return home and bring the dreadlock and any other paraphernalia that was used by her in the worship of spirits or of Buddha. I called our bible worker trainees to come and pray for the lady. When the dreadlock arrived the lady unwrapped it and began talking about it, at which point her voice changed to a male voice. I took the dreadlock from her and laid it on the floor. No sooner had I done this, a large green grasshopper flew in and landed on it. With the help of the lady, we set fire to the dreadlock, her waist charm which I had cut off with her permission, and the other paraphernalia her husband had brought. The sky was blue with just a hint of cloud on the northern horizon which is the direction of the ancient Angkor Wat Temple location. Many students prayed for this lady with the prayer session closed by myself. Shortly after, the lady again began talking in a male voice and it was quite obvious the lady was no longer in control of the conversation. This was a demonic spirit that had taken possession of her. I began ordering, in the name of Jesus, for this spirit to leave the lady. It had identified itself as Ta Essay, a local folk-being who supposedly is a protective character. I continued to order this evil spirit to leave and after about ten minutes it shook her legs and she became conscious again. She knew nothing of what had just transpired. I was new to this and unsure of how to proceed, so I silently talked to the Holy Spirit seeking counsel on what to do next. I heard the Holy Spirit tell me that the evil spirit had not left. I told the lady that the spirit had not left and ordered Ta Essay to leave. Immediately the evil spirit was in control again and this time moving the hands of the lady in a Khmer dance style, then pointing at the centre of the roof above us said, "The ruling spirit at Angkor Wat is angry with you". Instantly a bolt of lightning struck directly above us and we saw fire run around the edge of the roof of the building. Then, within moments, rain came from the north and it was coming in horizontally. The northern side of the building had no wall. Just twenty minutes before, the sky was blue. The students and I picked the lady up and moved her into the clinic room where we continued to pray and order the spirit out in the name of Jesus. After about fifteen minutes she came conscious again and told us she had seen a short man about 30 cm high with long hair, hands tied behind its back, leave her.

Now when I read in Revelation 13 that the second beast will bring fire down from the sky, I see that moment when the dragon, Satan, brought fire out of the sky and struck our building. Some may argue the lightning and storm were just coincidence, but having been in the middle of the whole story, I can tell you it was not coincidence.

The following day I had a counselling session with the lady and she told me the lump in her back that would move up and down was still there. My students and I prayed for her and I began ordering the spirit out that was causing this lump. A spirit began talking saying the lady's husband had cut the branches off their tree and that is why they were occupying her. They said they would leave if her husband would build them a spirit house and place it outside the house. Then they began telling the husband the dimensions of the spirit house. At that point I spoke saying, "Jesus does not allow you to live in a spirit house, leave now. The lady returned to consciousness and this time described seeing two small, long haired people leave her, each with their hands tied behind their backs. Satan and his evil host are most definitely powerful, but Jesus is much more powerful. In Matthew 8:7, 8, Jesus told the disciples to preach about the Kingdom of Heaven, to heal the sick, cast out evil spirits and even raise the dead. When the seventy returned with joy after an evangelistic campaign and told Jesus, even the devils are subject to us through Your name, Jesus replied I saw Satan as lightning fall from heaven Luke 10:17, 18. Today evil spirits are just as active as when Jesus walked the streets of Israel.

Demons Are Real

One of the lessons taught to the Bible worker trainees was "How to free oneself from pacts made with Satan". This class helps the students recall and claim the blood of Jesus to break past agreements or pacts made with evil spirits by way of false worship, habitual sin, curses, etc. Total freedom in Christ is emphasised as essential if one is to participate in deliverance ministry. Two of my students concerned me as the Holy Spirit was telling me they both had a pride problem. Four hours after the last class on deliverance ministry, one of these two men became demon possessed. Some students hurried to my house to report to me that the young man was rolling on the floor in agony with his arms and legs being twisted by unseen hands. I gathered the students around him and we began ordering the evil spirits out. It quickly became apparent that his possession was like the demoniacs of Gadara, a legion of spirits had moved in. As we knelt to pray for him and ordered the spirits out in the name of Jesus, the second of the two men I was concerned for, knelt beside me laying his hands on the legs of the young man, and began to quietly pray. He then began retching and gasping for air. I looked at him and saw a dark shadow around him and realised a demonic presence was taking control of him also. I asked some of the students to move him away and pray for him, while the rest of us prayed with the first victim ordering the evil spirits out. As each spirit left, their victim would scream loudly and faint as if dead. On two occasions he was screaming that they were throwing spears at him and he coughed up pools of fresh red blood for effect. Evil spirits are a nasty bunch of thugs who will do whatever it takes to try to scare those that intercede. Twenty four hours later, after numerous attacks from the spirits, I asked the young man what he had done to host a legion of spirits. He shared how he had made a pact with a band of evil spirits for protection, how he had murdered several people, marketed narcotics and dabbled in black magic, all this before becoming a Christian. He thought that at baptism he was free of his past, but it would appear that the past had not been properly dealt with, the pact had not been repented of and broken by claiming the blood of Jesus. This done, the attacks ceased and the young man went on to be a successful soul winner with Jesus.

The man who began retching also had unresolved problems in his life, including hate for his father-in-law, and a love of power. When I was able to pray with him it was evident that he was not alone. With the Holy Spirit's help, the problem areas in his life were identified, he humbled himself in repentance and sought forgiveness after which the shadow of an evil presence left him.

Praise God for two classic examples of the dangers of harbouring sin in one's life. As a result of that experience, our students understood better the importance of continually wearing the full armour of God, and their role of taking the name of Jesus into battle against the powers and principalities of this world.

Demons Are Mean

Bible worker training classes were over for the day and the students and I were standing around chatting when a motor bike pulled up outside the classroom with a couple in their early 50's. The woman needed to be helped off the bike as she was a cripple in one leg. We sat down on the steps of the building and Chien and her husband shared their story. For the past 14 years Chien had been suffering from paralysis in her right leg and troubled by demons. She had called upon many Kru Khmer (traditional healers) but was still not relieved. She recounted a story of one of the Kru Khmers chanting over her, causing her to cough up three live snakes that she watched slither away, but still relief had not come. She had set up three spirit shelves in her house to make offerings to the spirits hoping to appease them, but this was to no effect. Word had filtered out through the villages that the Christian God was powerful at casting out evil spirits so they had come to us to call on our God to help them. I explained that before helping her find relief for her problem I would need to teach her about Jesus, the One who had the power to help her. The mention of the name of Jesus obviously hit a touchy spot with one of the spirits she was dealing with as it took control of her and Chien transformed from being paralysed in one leg to needing six strong young men to hold her down. I had to revise my plans about how I would deal with this problem and immediately began ordering the evil spirit out in the name of Jesus. This took some time, but the spirit retreated for a time. Chien and her husband took up residence in our classroom and began participating in the classes. The demons would attack quite frequently, usually giving Chien supernatural strength. I remember being called during one attack, and on arrival found

Chien spinning like a ballerina on her normally crippled leg. After several days Chien asked me to go to her home, 35 km away, to burn her spirit shelves as she wanted to separate herself from her former life. Her husband and I travelled on my motorbike while Chien slept on a mat in the classroom. At the time we arrived at the house and gathered up the things to be burned, Wendy was teaching a class with the Bible worker trainees. All of a sudden Chien sat up in the classroom with sweat running down her face crying loudly, 'they are burning me'. Wendy and the students gathered around her and began ordering out the spirit and it left. The following morning Chien's toes on one foot had burn blisters on them.

The attacks continued, manifesting in various ways. One evening Chien's abdomen began to rapidly swell until it looked like she was full term in a pregnancy with twins. We laid our hands on her abdomen and prayed, and as we prayed her abdomen deflated to normal size. As soon as we stopped praying, the abdomen inflated as large as before. This time we ordered the spirit to leave and her abdomen returned to normal size and stayed that way.

One day the students were asking me why when they ordered the spirits out nothing happened, but when I ordered them out they left even if only temporarily. I did not have an answer for them. The next morning I had prepared from the Desire of Ages the chapter to be presented as our morning worship, but as I walked to the classroom, I heard the Holy Spirit tell me I should not present what I had prepared but should speak about Achan. I presented that worship on Achan who had a secret sin that affected all Israel. During the worship, the Holy Spirit made me aware that I needed to give the

Achan's in the classroom time to confess. I made this known to the students and to my surprise students started coming forward, mostly two by two, and confessing to each other the disunity between them and asking for forgiveness. At one point my most on-fire student got up and apologised for his fervent loud prayers which were prayed with a proud heart. I sat there on the floor astonished that there was so much discord between these Bible Worker trainees, at the same time praising God for what He was doing in the hearts of these students. After worship I went home for breakfast, returning about an hour later for morning classes. What I found was an excited group of students. An evil spirit had attacked Chien while they were eating breakfast. This time when they ordered the evil spirit to leave her it left immediately. That morning was to be a lesson neither I nor they would ever forget.

Things progressed until there was apparently just one demon calling itself the eight arm god; it stubbornly refused to leave when ordered out in the name of Jesus. Chien and I began exploring issues in her life that may be giving this spirit the authority to stay. She shared with me a tragedy that had happened to her family not long before the demonic trouble began. Her teenage daughter had drowned. Chien had blamed herself for not being there to help save her daughter and as we discussed this, it became apparent that Chien was carrying heavy guilt for the death of her daughter. I led her to see that she was not complicit in her daughter's death and to seek forgiveness from Jesus for condemning herself. Having done this, I once more ordered the spirit out in the name of Jesus. This time there were no manifestations of power, the spirit had quietly left as its authority had now been revoked. Chien was so grateful to Jesus for what

He had done for her. With the departure of the demon she regained full use of her right leg again. This story played out over a couple of weeks. Our students, who were taught deliverance ministry as a part of their training, had witnessed first hand the power of Jesus' name to set Satan's captives free.

When dealing with evil spirits, there is no place for dialogue with them. They are deceptive and prone to lying. They will act up in a multitude of ways with the goal of distracting or discouraging those who are interceding on behalf of their victim. Our role, as the intercessor, is to call on the name of Jesus for the freedom of the victim. Beyond that it is important that we lead the delivered person to Christ and they fill their life with Him. Failure to do so may result in the formerly demonised person worse off than before deliverance (See Matthew 12:43-45).

Intercessory Prayer

I have come to understand the purpose of intercessory prayer is to help me learn to love others as much as God loves them. He wants me to desire their salvation as much as He desires their salvation. Only when we labour in prayer for another can we truly begin to understand the heart of God.

God used Korn, a married Cambodian Buddhist lady, to teach us much in this area of the Christian walk. Although still young, Korn was suffering severely from a malignant bone cancer growing on her face. As we visited her daily, it was obvious that her relatives and friends feared that her cancer was contagious and avoided going near her. Loving her as Christ loves her meant sitting with her, holding her hand, speaking encouraging words with her and praying for her. We took her a small cassette player with tapes of the dramatised New Testament in Khmer language. Korn would listen to the tapes in our absence. Each day as we visited her, and did our best to love her as Jesus would love her, she grew in her understanding of her new found friend and Saviour. We pleaded with God for her healing and did all we could to foster that healing, but the cancer progressively grew worse. While we saw no physical healing miracle, a greater miracle was taking place in Korn's life. Korn grew to love Jesus because of what He has done, is doing and will do for her. She found peace, forgiveness and joy with the knowledge of eternal life. The cancer took Korn's life but it could not take from her the new found love of God. Korn died with the hope of a cancer-free resurrection together with eternal life.

As Korn's faith grew, our faith struggled. Jesus had told His disciples to preach the Gospel, heal the sick, cast out evil spirits and raise the dead (Matthew 10:7,8). Jesus said, ask what you desire, in my name, and it will given to you (John 14:14). We desired Korn's healing and pleaded with God to grant our selfless desire in-line with His promise, but He apparently failed to keep His promise. We now believe that our desire, while being well meaning, was not what God desired, it was not what was truly going to bring honour to God, it was not what was eternally best for Korn. Korn's husband, family and friends were all Buddhist. If she had been miraculously healed, she most likely would have experienced considerable family and cultural pressure to abandon her new love for Jesus and may have backslidden like so many others we have seen. What God desired most for Korn was to grant her eternal life. We now believe that God, in His foreknowledge, could see the pressures that Korn would be subject to and chose to free her of that crisis by letting her sleep until the day of resurrection. God loved Korn enough to deny our intercessory prayer for her healing, knowing that by denying our request He could grant Korn our eternal friendship in His Kingdom. Korn is one of many whom we have seen transition from sickness to death, and from spiritual death to spiritual life. On the day of resurrection (1 Thessalonians 4:14-17) we will be united with those we have interceded for, never to be separated again. Through these experiences we have come to better understand the heart of God, and learned to love the salvation of a soul more than desiring the physical healing of a soul. We still pray for God to heal people and many times we have seen God miraculously work that healing, but we now understand that God's highest motive is always to grant eternal life at what ever the cost.

I have come to understand the purpose of intercessory prayer is to help me learn to love others as much as God loves them. He wants me to desire their salvation as much as He desires their salvation. Only when we labour in prayer for another can we truly begin to understand the heart of God.

When the Holy Spirit Speaks

A high day was unfolding at Wat Preah Yesu. Our bush hospital/clinic was to be opened with the village and commune leaders together with many local villagers joining us for the occasion. A visiting American optometrist was also present to provide free eye glasses to those in need. I had ventured into town on my 175cc two stroke motorbike to get some last minute supplies. On my return I was hurrying so as not to be late. From the main road I could see a group of villagers walking down the sandy road leading to the clinic. I decided to save time by cutting across the dry rice fields, making use of the opportunity to show the villagers walking along the road how I could jump the motorbike over a rice field bund. It was shortly after this thought had crossed my mind, I heard a still small voice say 'if you jump you will crash'. There was no reason why I should crash, I had done this many times before when no one was watching. Ignoring the voice and traveling at 75 km/hour I directed my front wheel toward the bund. As I was almost at the bund I realised I had made a mistake in alignment and instead of a bund with a gentle crescent shaped curve I was about to hit a bund that had square edges. I knew then that this was not going to end well, but it was too late to make corrections or slow down. The front wheel hit the bund, turned skyward together with me and the rest of the bike until gravity took over with the front wheel hitting ground first and the bike and me following after. The bike's steering was knocked out of alignment, my chest and left foot hurt, but what was hurt the most was my pride. I had crashed not far from the people who I proudly wanted to show off to. I lifted my prideful aching body from on top of the motorbike, picked up the bike, and got out of there as quickly as my twisted steering would let me.

God is so gracious. He kept my pain to a very tolerable level. The clinic opening went well and the morning eye clinic blessed many people with glasses. Lunch passed and I limped back over to the clinic for the afternoon eye clinic. About twenty minutes in, when things were quieting down, the pain in my foot began to be excruciating. I excused myself and limped home crawling up the steps to the bedroom. The pain was so bad it was making me feel nauseous. I laid on the mat and confessed to God my pride and foolishness, asking for forgiveness and praised Him for His graciousness in letting me get through this much of the day without excessive pain. While my ribs hurt, the pain was nothing compared to the foot. I asked God to heal the foot and shortly after fell asleep. I awoke about an hour later to an almost painless foot. It was now obvious that my ribs hurt. I stood up and could walk fine without significant pain. God had honoured my repentance with healing. The ribs continued to hurt for a couple of weeks. I believe God was using the pain as gentle reminder that God is not honoured by pride.

On another occasion I was travelling home mid-Sunday afternoon, hot and hungry after working all morning on the renovation of a house which we planned to use as a small church. As I was approaching the road leading to home, I heard that same small voice again, saying, 'Go to town'. Town was another 6 km down the road. I was tired, hot, thirsty and hungry, but I had now learned the lesson that when the Holy Spirit speaks, it is prudent to listen and act immediately on the Spirit's request. I proceeded to town wondering what God would have me do when I arrived. Coming into town I silently prayed asking where was I to go. In the Holy Spirit's usual short, concise way, I heard just one word, 'Hospital'. After parking my motorbike at the hospital, I was thinking through who I might know that was at the hospital. I remembered a woman who had come to our clinic and Wendy had referred her to the provincial hospital where she had been diagnosed with cancer. I sought her out and on finding her realised this woman did not have much time left before she would breathe her last breath. It was now clear why I had been sent; this lady did not know Jesus and her salvation was in the balance with just a little time left. I knelt beside her bed and for the next half hour shared with her what Jesus had done at the cross to offer her the hope of eternal life. With tears rolling down her cheeks, she gave her life to Jesus. One hour later she breathed the last breath until Jesus returns and she hears His mighty call to arise. That afternoon, if I had allowed self to get the victory and ignored the Holy Spirit, the Kingdom of heaven would have been deprived of a daughter whose sins had been paid for with the life of Jesus. I wonder how many times I have ignored the Holy Spirit, depriving a lost soul of the knowledge of God and eternal life. Thank God for His patience and grace.

Fear God, not the gods

Cambodia is a majority Buddhist country and Buddhist temple complexes (Wat) are found throughout the country. The word Wat means a place of moral teaching. Usually a Wat will occupy at least a hectare of land and have a central temple, a multi-purpose building known as the Sala (school) Chann (word for when Buddhist monks eat), accommodation for monks, numerous family stupas to hold the bone fragments of the dead, and a wall around it with two or more gateways. Outside the wall, but usually adjoining, will be accommodation for elderly females who sign in as Buddhist nuns for a period of time (often six months) and a crematorium. A primary school may also be located just outside of the Wat. In a well established Wat, tall trees will create a somewhat park like feeling. The Wat is a community meeting point where much social interaction can take place, especially on religious holidays.

The Wat is not the only centre of religious activity as many family related ceremonies and merit earning ceremonies happen in the community at family homes, especially with respect to weddings, and funerals. Monks will daily walk through the villages in the morning collecting donations of food and money, with the giver kneeling on the side of the road, before the monks, to receive a chanted blessing.

The high imposing temples and regular religious activities give the visitor a sense that the Khmer people are religiously very Buddhist. However, only when you get to know the language can you really get to know the people, at which time you discover the people are more superstitious than religious and more animist and worshippers of their ancestors than they are Buddhist. Buddhism has typically been a very syncretistic religion absorbing religious practices that it should have replaced, the result being a very confusing package of beliefs. To add to this, culture and religious practices are so intertwined that it is hard to discern what is culture and what is religion. This I found to be a major stumbling block as I shared Jesus with the Khmer people. After church planting for a couple of years in Siem Reap town, I arrived at a false conclusion that the only way to truly convert a Khmer Buddhist person to Christianity was to extract them from their religion and their culture. I had not heard about contextualisation, nor did I see how it could be possible to incorporate what I considered Buddhist cultural practices into Christianity without compromising the Biblical teachings. It was after this low point, when the Khmer language began to be understandable, that my professor, the Holy Spirit, began to help me see that culture and religion can be separated. And just because Buddhist practice is Buddhist and very foreign from my western Christian forms, does not mean that it does not have a biblical precedent. Gradually the option of contextualising Christianity in Cambodia became not only a possibility but a significant opportunity. A whole new world of evangelism and subsequent discipleship opened before me.

Khmer people worship barefoot and on the ground, legs folded to oneside so as not to imitate the lotus position of the Buddha. Moses and Joshua were told by God to take off their shoes because they were standing on holy ground. The biblical worshipper is often described as having their face to the ground. Many Khmer religious practices appear to be far closer to the biblical practice than western Christian practices. Christian Khmer people take their shoes off as a sign of respect before entering a church, or a private dwelling.

While attending various religious ceremonies in people's homes, we observed that at the height of the worship activities when the monks were chanting, many of the people, with hands in a praying position in front of them and legs folded to one-side, were busy talking to each other, obviously detached from the religious activity. In contrast, when visiting Buddhist temples, people were very reverent. An idea came to me that if Christians worshipped in a building that architecturally was similar to the Buddhist temple, they may also behave reverently. I followed up this idea by building a full-sized church in Buddhist temple style. The reverence result was disappointing, at which time I concluded that the architectural style was not the reason for the reverence, but rather the four meter high Buddha statue sitting in lotus position at one end of the temple was the actual reason for the reverence. It became apparent that Christian reverence is a result of respect, and respect comes when a worshipper knows who His God is and what His God is doing for him. While this experiment failed to induce reverence, it did result in a building that was ideal for worship in a tropical environment, and aesthetically pleasant to look at.

Another experiment I did at the Siem Reap City Adventist church, where traditionally the worshippers sat on plastic chairs, was to remove the chairs for a Sabbath worship program. The responses were interesting ranging from refusing to enter to worship through to a heightened worship experience. On interviewing people after the worship program, one adult member made this comment, 'Usually I feel like I am coming to church to learn because we sit on chairs, but today, without the chairs, it felt like I was worshipping God.

I now see that thoughtful contextualisation of Adventist religious practice is not only doable but enhances the quality of the worship experience, without compromising the teachings.

We Will Go

While volunteering as farm manager at Fulton College, Fiji, I heard God call me to pastoral ministry, but at the time had no idea how that could be possible. About fifteen months later, living in Siem Reap, Cambodia, that call became a reality as we shepherded a church plant in our new home.

However my vision of what God's calling meant and what God actually called me to, were quite different and only time would reveal how different. Several more years would pass before again hearing God speak, this time calling us to train lay people to be church planters. This would have been inconceivable to me four years before, when the call to pastoral work first came. In 1999, I shifted from being church planter and trainer of church planters, to being the pastor's pastor, or as we know it here, district pastor, as I took on the responsibility of ministering to those who we had trained as church planters. How is such a transition possible without formal training? The answer is the promise that we would go anywhere, do anything, for any length of time. Anything, although we did not know it when we made the promise, this also meant being the pastor of pastors. God is looking for hearts that are committed to work in partnership with Him. When God's throne is set up in a person's heart, God can do unimaginable things with that person's life.

I find teaching people from the word of God really exciting because as I teach, the Holy Spirit, my professor, takes me deeper into the word unfolding previously unseen truths. This happened very often while teaching the church planter trainees, but one particular event was to be life changing for me. I was in Thailand helping Pastor Scott Griswold with a training for senior pastors from around SouthEast Asia. The Holy Spirit led me to study John 13 to 17 at a level well beyond anything I had ever heard or understood before. This study of the words Christ spoke the night before His crucifixion, continues to be life transforming for me as the Holy Spirit reveals the depth of relationship God desires to have with people like you and me. John 17:23 spoke to me the deepest. "I in them, and thou in me, that they may be made perfect in one; and that the world may know that thou hast sent me, and hast loved them, as thou hast loved me." Here we have the Father in Jesus, Jesus in us, and as a result of God's presence in us, we become perfect as we unite together as one. The consequence of this is that the world comes to know about God.

As I studied this text my heart began rebelling against what I read. The text appeared to be saying that God the Father, and Jesus, both desired to have the same depth of relationship with me as they have with each other. Together with the Holy Spirit, they are the Trinity, three but one. What right do I, a sinner, have to be included in Their inner circle. But that is what Jesus said, the Father in Him, He in me. In desperation to resolve this unimaginable relationship with God, I turned to the writings of Mrs White on this subject and was shocked to find she understood this text to mean exactly that depth of relationship. Tears poured from deep within as I better understood that God the Father is not wanting to wait for me to walk through the pearly gates of New Jerusalem so He can be with me, but desires that relationship to begin immediately and wants a relationship far deeper than the picture rolls portray of His children sitting in a heavenly garden conversing with Jesus surrounded by gentle animals.

Today I understand that the Father, together with Jesus, and the Holy Spirit, want to dwell in the sanctuary of my heart. When Paul says, "It is no longer I that liveth but Christ that liveth in me" (Galatians 2:20), he is talking about that deep relationship. That relationship only becomes possible with the daily death of self. When I ask God to bless my plans, then self is still in charge, even if I am doing "God's work." If self is dead, I ask God to make known to me His plans for our day, and then go to work together with Him. The day takes on a whole new perspective when you see the reality of being in partnership with God, working together for the good of the Kingdom of Heaven, our kingdom. Our Kingdom, because Paul said we are joint heirs with Jesus (Romans 8:17). Jesus did not die for us so we could live eternally in a beautiful city playing with tame animals and walking on golden streets. He died so that we could be Kings and Priests reigning together with Him over the Kingdom of Heaven. Paul also gives us a glimpse into this when he says, 'we are seated together with Jesus in Heavenly places' (Ephesians 2:6). God can't wait for the second coming to have us reign together with Him, He wants that reality now. After nearly forty years of mission service, I am still learning that if I want to have a great day, I'll spend it with God doing what God wants to do.

Maybe the reason we are still waiting for the latter rain of the Holy Spirit in our lives is because we want the gift (the power) but not the Giver. It is logical to understand that if the Father, Son and Holy Spirit are reigning from within us, that already all power in heaven and earth is ours, because we are God's.

God is looking for hearts that are committed to work in partnership with Him. When God's throne is set up in a person's heart, God can do unimaginable things with that persons life.

Jesus did not die for us so we could live eternally in a beautiful city playing with tame animals and walking on golden streets. He died so that we could be Kings and Priests reigning together with Him over the Kingdom of Heaven.

Educate For Eternity

Adventist education had become an intrinsic part of who we are. We both spent time studying at Adventist schools, we met at a Seventh-day Adventist school and had grown closer to God as a result of being students in Seventh-day Adventist schools. But God had not called us to partner with Him in starting schools, at least that is what we thought. God had called us to plant a new church and train new Seventh-day Adventist Christians to be church planters. We were about to learn that just because God did not say to start schools, did not mean it was not on His list of things for us to do. The first awareness of this came as we were negotiating with one of the local commune leaders about the purchase of land. He suggested it would be good for us to start a school in the community he governed. We could ask, "Why didn't God tell us to do that?" In hindsight, I believe I now understand the wisdom of God better. I was an educator, and I had worked in Seventh-day Adventist Mission schools for seven years. For me, starting a school was going to be much easier than training laypeople to be church planters. God did not want us side-tracked doing what came naturally. His wisdom was expressed in silence until the time was right. That time came after the first Bible worker training program. The children of the poorest of the poor came asking for education because their families could not afford to send them to the government schools. One of our converts from our local village had completed the church planter training, she had a grade two education and a passion to teach. We gave Pber a veranda, a board and a group of students to whom she was to teach basic Khmer literacy. We had stepped into the river and there would be no turning back. Pber is still teaching in our school twenty-three years later, only now she is our sewing teacher.

The literacy school on a verandah morphed into a primary school with classrooms, and then we added a boarding component for Seventh-day Adventist children from the rural churches. Today the school is bilingual, offering kindergarten to grade 12, having an enrolment of 240 students. The boarding students number just over 100 with all but three from Seventh-day Adventist homes. The school has become the centre of evangelism for our local communities, with most of our high school students from Buddhist families giving their hearts to Jesus before they leave the school.

The school has outlasted the church planter training program but could not have existed without that program. Our original national teachers were mostly drawn from the pool of lay people who completed the four month training. None of them were trained educators but all of them were willing to allow the Holy Spirit to impart to them the gift of teaching. These national workers were joined by foreign volunteers who came at their own expense to teach in the English language. Some of these volunteers were as young as sixteen when they arrived. This combined Spirit-led effort has resulted in many Cambodian Seventh-day Adventist young people graduating from grade 12 and going on to study in universities. Many of these young people have taught in our schools while pursuing university degrees. Today we have eighteen national teaching staff, sixteen are former students from our school. Many of our high school graduates have left to teach in other Adventist schools around Cambodia. To see what God has done is to see an ongoing miracle. Today I am the only university qualified teacher on our staff of twenty-four, but that is no issue to God.

Ten years ago we believed God was calling us to begin a second school about forty kilometres from our campus. With funding from the Marienhöhe school in Germany, we built three classrooms on the block of land across the road from our Tani church. The Tani school continues to be a feeder school, currently offering grades 1-4.

Every school day begins with a forty-five minute Bible class except grades 11 and 12. The grade 11 and 12 students know their Bible well so we teach them evangelism and give them opportunity to practice what they learn by either conducting an evangelistic program at one of the local Seventh-day Adventist churches, or partnering with foreign evangelists. Medical evangelism is also taught under the subject name health, with opportunities provided to run health expos in local communities. These same students also learn how to be teachers with the grade 12 students getting practice in the classroom teaching primary school mathematics in English. To round out our senior students education, they are also assigned with supervising the boarding students during their after school work time. This educational program for our senior students creates a bridge for them to transition from being students to being colleagues in the work of God.

Four fundamental beliefs drive education in our schools. The first is that God wants all of His children to receive a truly Seventh-day Adventist education. The second is that God will help pay for His children's education if the parents cannot afford to pay. The third is that children need to receive academic education together with vocational education. The fourth sees the education provided as preparing children to be future Kings and Priests of God who will reign with Him for eternity. Our teachers understand that they have the responsibility of teaching a unique group of students, the children of the King of kings.

As we have grown in our understanding of the first belief we have tested the second belief to the max. Believing that every Seventh-day Adventist child should have an Seventh-day Adventist education has meant us trusting God to pay for much or all of their education. The majority of our Cambodian church members are very poor. To be a full paying boarding student in our school currently costs US$640 per year. That is more than many families earn in a year. For this reason we ask Seventh-day Adventist parents to pay US$170 per year as a heavily subsidised tuition fee. Even at US$170 per year many are still unable to pay, so we add their children's tuition expenses to the boarding fee and put it on God's bill. Previously we would only accept boarding students ten years of age or older, but this school year with falling orphan numbers, we have opened the orphan homes for six to nine year old children from Seventh-day Adventist families. This provides family based accommodation and meals to these young children while allowing them to get an early start on their bilingual Seventh-day Adventist education. Some may argue that these young students should be at home with their parents. While that is the ideal, often their parents are not at home to take care of them. An additional problem is that many of the parents are illiterate, or barely literate, so family worship does not happen. Some students will beg us to let them stay during the holidays even if they have to work. The reason is they know that food at home is going to be rice and fish, two meals a day, and they are going to lose weight while on vacation. Providing these children with three nutritious meals daily, morning and evening worships, and supervised care in a Christian environment, gives them a good academic and spiritual boost.

The vocational component of our education program helps our students develop skills in agriculture, art and crafts, sewing, cooking, computers, music, and multi-media, providing a well rounded education that helps a child explore their strengths and pursue a career suited to their gifts and abilities.

As founder and principal of the school, I have the unique experience of working with teachers who I first got to know when they were in our primary school. If the Gospel is to go to all the world in this generation, this generation needs a truly Seventh-day Adventist education to prepare them to accomplish this monumental task.

God Tricked Us

Have you ever made a promise to God, but then back tracked on your promise. We confess we are guilty. We said we would do anything, but when it came to running an orphanage, that was not included in our anything. Praise God that He has ways of setting up circumstances so that the word *anything* is inclusive of everything. Now before explaining, you may remember how God orchestrated a visit to India for us where we visited orphanages, never thinking that we would be involved in establishing an orphanage some 16 years later. Then in 1996 as we were planning to buy land for the training centre, a friend by the name of Marshall Smith offered to give us some money to buy extra land where He could start an orphanage in the future. A seed was sown but we never pictured ourselves harvesting the fruit of it. God used the bush clinic Wendy operated to bring to our attention the plight of children being orphaned by HIV AIDS and from that we gained our daughter Ly. Still the concept of an orphanage was in Marshall's hands until it wasn't. Marshall married in Japan and decided Japan was a huge, virtually untouched mission field to which he should dedicate his life. Now we have land, we see a need, but we are unwilling to proceed. Our excuses were, we are church planting, training church planters, overseeing church plants and developing a school, while trying to raise three children. Working behind the scenes, God was preparing to hold us to our promise. A family from the USA visited and expressed sincere interest in establishing and running the orphanage. At the same time we received a large sum of money from the deceased estate of a late friend in Australia. Seeing God's providence we moved forward doing land fill for the orphanage site and constructing the first of what would be seven orphanage duplex houses. We also began processing the paperwork to operate a licensed orphanage. We were facilitating so that someone else could run the orphanage. The ball was now rolling and gaining momentum to the point of no turning back. It was then that God made His move putting us in checkmate. The family from the USA lost the support of their local church and withdrew their offer to come and run the orphanage. It was only then that we realised God had set us up, and in hindsight oh how thankful we are that He did. We had made a promise and God was going to hold us to our promise for our own good.

Twenty-one years have passed since that life-changing news that the orphanage was going to be our baby. Nearly 300 children have come and gone from the orphanage in the ensuing years. Most entered the waters of baptism before they left. Many of our current staff of more than sixty Cambodian nationals came to us as children and babies in need of love and knowing Jesus. God took that orphanage and the children in it and used them to mould and shape our lives in preparation for eternal loving service in the Kingdom of Heaven. Today, the Orphanage goes under the name Butterfly Paradise Orphanage, and is home to 24 orphan children, but at its peak provided love, shelter and education to 196 children.

We established the orphanage on the family model, a husband and wife taking care of up to sixteen children. They were big families, but for the most part, happy families. Management of each family was handled by the foster parents for that family. This model was a gift from God, allowing Wendy and I to enjoy the children without having to expend much time in parenting.

While we only have two biological children, we have hundreds who call us mum and dad, and those who call us grandma and grandpa are increasing with every passing year. How foolish we were to try to escape the promise just because we thought we were too busy. As always, God knew what would be best for us and manipulated circumstances so we could have the best He could offer.

Death Is a Rest

As evening drew on, and weariness had set in, I received an urgent phone call from a dorm student's father. He requested I drive the 316 km to Phnom Penh that night to take his teenage daughter, Chamneng, home to Oddar Meanchey Province. She was dying of Leukaemia. He had taken her to Phnom Penh in the hope that maybe something could be done for her, but it was to no avail. If she died in the hospital, it was going to cost him US$500 to get her body transported in an ambulance the 500 km home. In Cambodia it is very bad luck to transport a corpse in your private vehicle. If you can convince someone to do so, it will cost a lot of money and require a spirit cleansing ceremony for the vehicle after the fact. I apologised to him that I could not make the journey that night as I was far too tired to make the drive safely. I then assured him I would make the six hour drive the following day.

Arriving at the hospital in Phnom Penh, I found Chamneng unconscious and close to death. I sat with her, holding her hand and quietly praying while the father worked on the papers to release her from the hospital. Shortly after, her heart stopped beating. Despite protests from the girl's father and aunty, the medical staff proceeded to resuscitate her. The staff finally agreed to take her off life support and allow her to be lifted into the passenger seat of my car. Chamneng's heart stopped beating shortly after. It was now five o'clock in the evening, and I had to drive across Phnom Penh in rush hour traffic with a corpse sitting in the passenger seat of the car. We left her face uncovered so as to not draw undue attention. We arrived at our campus shortly before midnight, and rested till morning before making the final leg of the journey.

The following morning her body was lifted onto the back tray of the orphanage truck and students and staff climbed aboard ready for the three hour drive to Chamneng's home where she would be buried in a simple grave on the family's farm. In Cambodia, foreigners are not allowed to be issued with truck licences, but as I had done many times before, I took the drivers seat, hoping I would not get stopped for a licence check. As we passed through Samrong town, the police waved me over and asked me to get out of the truck and go to their table and show my licence. While I was disembarking from the truck, the policeman began asking the Khmer staff and students on the back of the truck where they were going. They pointed to the body wrapped up on the floor of the truck and answered, "to a funeral". The policeman turned back to me and invited me to continue our journey without licence check. I breathed a silent prayer of thanks and continued our journey to take Chamneng to her funeral.

In Cambodian Buddhist thinking, the funeral is the most important event in a person's life, even though they miss it because they are dead. For Khmer Buddhists, the body is cremated after an elaborate ceremony that may stretch over several days. Usually the ashes will be placed in an urn and kept in a family stupa at the local temple. For Cambodian Christians, funerals are often a problem, having nowhere to cremate or bury. To help solve this problem, our local church built a stupa in the shape of a cross next to the church, and made it available to all Cambodian Christians who would like to intern the ashes of their dead on our campus. We also have a graveyard behind our school, where, at the time of writing, forty people are resting in their graves till Jesus comes again.

Death in countries like Cambodia, is by no means sterile as it is in most developed countries. Family members take care of the body at the family home until cremation or burial. The family washes the body and prepares it for its final resting place. If a cremation is done, and there is no facility for cremations, they are done in a field with the body cremated on a funeral pyre. We have done this numerous times on our campus. If a deceased Christian has a majority of Buddhist relatives, it is likely that they are going to want the body cremated.

The funeral is an important time for the family of the deceased to gather together and remember the life of their loved one. The grieving process is aided as the family participate together in this farewell process. For Buddhists, there is no rest after death. If the funeral is not done well they believe the person's spirit will likely take up a cleaner's role at the local pagoda until it is released to the next life. If the funeral is adequate, the spirit will be reincarnated to suffer in a new life only to die again, this cycle being repeated endlessly. Reaching Nirvana is their only hope to escape suffering. Many believe Nirvana is becoming one with the universe or to put it another way, to experience eternal non-existence. Christian funerals are usually attended by the Buddhist relatives of the deceased. This provides an evangelistic opportunity to share a better hope of life after death than Buddhism offers.

My favourite Bible verse when conducting funerals is found at the end of the third angels message in Revelation 14:13. "And I heard a voice from heaven saying unto me, Write, Blessed are the dead which die in the Lord from henceforth: Yea, saith the Spirit, that they may rest from their labours; and their works do follow them." The word rest has so much joy attached to it after a life of suffering on this earth. I love the way God chose to have the next verse, Revelation 14:14, announce the second coming of Jesus as the harvest: the resurrection of the dead and the transformation of the righteous living. I look forward to that day when my Khmer brothers and sisters, who are at rest, will rise to eternal life. If God chooses to delay His coming, so that more may be saved, and in the meantime I go to my rest, I hope to be buried alongside my brothers and sisters in Christ, in the graveyard behind the school, to await that joyous day.

Volunteerism

In the 39 years we have worked in the mission field, we have had the privilege of working with many volunteers and have volunteered ourselves. Volunteers are a special group of people who are willing to make a sacrifice for the Kingdom of Heaven. For some, the sacrifice is a few days and others it is a lifetime. All make a contribution to the advancement of the Kingdom of God.

I have learned to characterise volunteers into four categories, the helpers: the helpers that need help, those that need help, and the tourists. The helpers are those who come with a strong relationship with God and are equipped to dig in and make a difference. The helpers that need help also have a strong relationship with God but due to lack of experience, negative past experiences, or misconceptions, need spiritual help to continue their Christian growth. Those that need help, are those who God has chosen to send as volunteers primarily to help them see their own personal needs, and be ministered to by fellow Christians, and most importantly by the Holy Spirit. The final group, the tourists, are those who are taking advantage of a ministry to meet their own personal agenda.

As a ministry leader, the first group are the kind of volunteer I naturally would prefer. People who I can assign a task and know that they are going to give it their best, with me investing a minimal amount of time in helping them fulfil that task. But the word ministry is about helping others, whether they be a beneficiary or a volunteer. I have come to understand that part of the ministry God has given us, is to minister to volunteers.

For a few volunteers, no matter how much is done to accommodate their perceived needs, it will never be enough. We believe that these volunteers are sent by God to help us with our own personal character development. Revelation 14 describes God's last day people as being patient. Demanding volunteers are an excellent grindstone on which to develop patience.

When volunteers come as couples or families, the dynamics get more complex, especially when volunteering is the passion of one, but the spouse is going along just to keep the other happy. This usually ends miserably for all concerned. Food, climate, and housing all contribute to a volunteer's positive or negative experience. Less open-minded volunteers, may find the challenges too great leading to their early termination of service. Many who volunteer are looking for their God-given calling in life, and may decide ahead of the agreed service period that they have found their calling, and move on to follow that call. I have also discovered that a volunteer rejected by another ministry may turn out to be perfect for our ministry, so I don't automatically reject the rejected.

For the most part, volunteers return to their home country with a greater appreciation for those who have less than themselves, and a greater heart for continuing to support mission financially and through prayer. The volunteers' positive impact made through development of friendships, and their encouraging others in their walk with God, is sure to have an eternal impact for the Kingdom of Heaven.

Much of the success of our ministry, particularly in the area of education, has been the result of hundreds of self-sacrificing, short and long-term volunteers.

Orphan Stories

In Exodus 22:22, God told the Israelites not to mistreat any widow or orphan. Most of us would understand that to mean, I should not exploit a widow or orphan, but I think God was thinking at a much more personal level than that. If we know a child is an orphan or vulnerable and we ignore the needs of that child, have we not actually mistreated that child? In Matthew 25, Jesus talks about feeding the hungry, clothing the naked and providing shelter for the homeless. Among others He is including orphans and vulnerable children. As disciples of Jesus, it should be our automatic, Spirit-given instinct to intervene in the lives of such children for the glory of God. We could personally intervene, or facilitate our local church's intervention. Only by Spirit-led intervention is that child going to experience the love of God and catch a glimmer of hope for this life and eternal life to come. Here I will share with you two stories of children who came into the care of our orphanage and how experiencing the love of God transformed their lives. I will use pseudonyms to protect their identity. As the word Samnang is Khmer for Lucky, and Samnang is lucky because the God of Heaven loves her, I will use Samnang as the name for the first girl's story.

Samnang's parents had both died, leaving Samnang an only child, an orphan. At two years of age Samnang was living with her aunty and uncle. Samnang's aunty and uncle lived on the edge of a border town called Osmach, a town known for its hundreds of prostitutes. Wendy and I felt impressed to go to the town of Osmach and enquire of the authorities whether in the town there were orphans and vulnerable children that needed a home. They told us about a family that lived within sight of a government school, but none of the five children went to school. We investigated that family and accepted all five children into the orphanage. These children had a mother but were highly vulnerable. They also told us of a two year old that had been apparently sold by her aunty to a family that was much better off. They had heard rumours that this two year old child was being abused by making it eat with the pigs and sometimes sleep with the pigs. They had no hard evidence so could not intervene. We left them our contact information and told them to contact us if anything changed. Wendy and I prayed that if God wanted this child in our orphanage, that He would intervene. Two weeks later I received a call from the Osmach authorities to tell me to come and pick up the child they had told me about. With our only transportation a 250cc motorbike, I climbed on the motorbike and began the 164 km journey to Osmach, arriving four hours later after a very bumpy ride. A local official took me to the home of the girl's aunty. The home was a small low thatched house. There were six small children running around, five wearing one piece of clothing each and one little two year old girl, naked. The aunty told me what had happened. She had heard the rumour about her niece Samnang, so she had gone to the home of Samnang's foster parents and asked for her back. Her request was denied. She returned home, sending her soldier husband with his AK 47 rifle to make the same request. This time the request was granted. The little naked girl I had seen running around, was Samnang. The family was so poor they could not even afford to clothe their own children properly. Official paperwork completed, Samnang's aunty called two of her children taking pants off one and a shirt off the other, and put the clothes on Samnang. I picked Samnang up, sat her in front of me on the seat of the motorbike. We began what was to be a nine hour journey home. I could not ride fast as Samnang would be bounced off. Everything went well until Samnang began to fall asleep. I realised I had not thought this through very well. Riding a motorbike with a two year old for 164 km along a rough road was not a journey that demonstrated wisdom. I took a Cambodian scarf out of my back pack and tied it around Samnang and I, hoping it would prevent her from falling off, it did little to help the situation. I then did what I should have done to begin with, I prayed for wisdom. I was surprised by the simplicity of the Holy Spirits answer- 'button her into your shirt'. I unbuttoned my shirt, wrapped it around her torso and head and buttoned it back up. She did not cry or struggle and quickly went back to sleep, safe in her improvised cocoon. It was nine at night when we arrived at the orphanage. I had spent thirteen hours on the motorbike that day. I was exhausted, but grateful for a safe journey and a new child for Christ to love through us.

Today Samnang is a beautiful young lady who loves the Lord. She is happily married to one of our teachers. After leaving school she worked in Butterfly Paradise for quite sometime until she gave birth to a son named Benjamin. The life that was and the life that is are a world apart. Our intervention, the love of the house parents and teachers and the financial support from donors have made Samnang's life a life of joy, where it otherwise may have been a life of hell.

Hadassah was born to a very ill mother infected with HIV. Very early in the life of Hadassah she was fostered to a well meaning family. Hadassah became sick with serious diarrhoea and needed hospitalisation. The family fearing Hadassah had contracted the HIV virus from her mother, abandoned her in the district hospital. Five months old, abandoned, but not forgotten, God sent the church planter in that town to the hospital to visit the sick. The doctors told him of the plight of Hadassah and he called me. The hospital was ninety kilometres away in another province and I guess I was busy as I told him I did not see how I could help. The next day he called to say the doctors had asked him to take Hadassah to our orphanage. I had the inspired impression that God was not pleased with me the day before when I had shrugged off the need of this child. I told the church planter to get in a share taxi and bring the child. Hadassah with no name and no birthdate became a resident in the nursery for babies. Hadassah was not HIV positive and was doing well in the nursery when two events would bring us together in a unique way. I had a motorcycle accident right in front of my house leaving my right foot with such pain that I did not want to make the journey to hospital resigning myself to the fact that bones were broken and I needed to take a two week vacation with my foot off the ground. That same day, Hadassah's carer had to go to stay in the hospital due to illness. Wendy brought baby Hadassah to the house, somewhat annoyed at me for breaking my foot and said to me 'you have nothing to do for a couple of weeks, so you can care for Hadassah,' which I did. A special bond developed between us that remains to this day. Hadassah has since got to know both of her grandmothers, and her extended family, but lives in our orphanage and is completing her studies at our school. She aspires to go to Australia to do further study before becoming a missionary.

Hundreds of stories could be written here of children whose lives have been eternally transformed because of the intervention of caring people. Family based orphanage care is one way of providing for children like Hadassah and Samnang. Foster care and adoption are other ways of caring that don't require infrastructure and administration. When we love another's child as if they were our own, we will better understand the heart of God who has adopted us into His family.

When we love another's child as if they were our own, we will better understand the heart of God who has adopted us into His family.

For Any Length of Time: 2005 to Eternity

In 1995 when God spoke to me about His plan for our lives, it was like looking into a time tunnel that extended only as far as 2005, beyond that was darkness. Now as I write, it is 2024, nearly twenty years beyond the darkness of the time tunnel. Today it is as if we stand on a broad open sunlit meadow, covered in flowers. The meadow is Cambodia and the flowers are the fruit that has come out of the partnership in ministry God called us to in 1995. The church planting, medical missionary work, Bible worker training, schools, orphanage, media ministry and personal witness have all contributed to the growth of the church across Cambodia. Being located in one place with an expanding ministry has given us a unique glimpse into the impact the lives of one family can have on the Kingdom of heaven, when they unite with God in spreading the good news.

One of the most frightening thoughts that from time to time passes through my mind, is this: "What if we had said NO when God called us to Cambodia (given the circumstances NO was the logical and safest answer)? What if we had said No when God called us to incarnational ministry at the cost of everything we had saved and owned? Whenever I am at a large Adventist gathering here in Cambodia, the answer to that question is rather unnerving. Many, and sometimes most in the gathering, would simply not be there. If we had said no to God, many would not have had opportunity to hear and accept the Gospel. That number grows every year as our Cambodian brothers and sisters who heard the gospel as a result of our family saying yes, share that same gospel with others.

This is all possible because God called us and blessed us with His presence, wisdom, courage, determination, and faith. The fruit is also the result of ourselves being willing to accept the call. Other significant factors to fruit bearing are the prayers and financial gifts of many, as well as the gift of time that many foreign volunteers have given. Equally essential to this success has been the close partnership with the Cambodia Adventist Mission, beginning with Pastor Daniel Walter and continued with each successive mission president.

God has brought together a network of people to make our ministry a success. Without this network, we could not have achieved anything of significance. Jesus spoke of how this success is to be achieved in John 17:21, "That they all may be one; as thou, Father, art in me, and I in thee, that they also may be one in us: that the world may believe that thou hast sent me." When God's people unite as one IN CHRIST, the world takes notice of who Jesus is. When the organised church, lay ministries and individual lay people, unite in Christ with a common trust, with a common purpose, and a common wealth, it will become clear to the world that Jesus was sent by the Father to bring love and harmony back into a world that is divided by fear and lack of trust.

The gospel is going to the world, but how much more could the Holy Spirit achieve through God's people if they would put aside their turf wars, and stop trying to keep the money to themselves. Instead they could be uniting in Christ under His leadership to get the job done and go home.

When the organised church, lay ministries and individual lay people, unite in Christ with a common trust, with a common purpose, and a common wealth, it will become clear to the world that Jesus was sent by the Father to bring love and harmony back into a world that is divided by fear and lack of trust.

Building on Faith

A ministry campus needs buildings to do effective ministry. Buildings can be make-shift, as were the first homes we put up, or they can be permanent, well constructed buildings that testify that God is in His work long-term. Buildings can be designed and erected for current needs or can be designed with expansion of God's work in mind. Over the past 27 years we have designed and overseen the construction of dozens of buildings with various purposes. On our Wat Preah Yesu campus we have almost one hectare (about two acres of roof coverage). That all started with a limited understanding of God's purpose and a growing faith in His ability and willingness to supply.

When Joshua and the people of Israel walked into the promised land of Canaan, it appeared to be an impossibility. The Jordan river was in flood and there were no bridges. God's command was go forward and it was the priests carrying the ark of the covenant which were to go first. The ark represented both God's presence and His promise. The Ark being at the front gave the message that God was leading, which he had done through the pillar of fire and the cloud for the past 40 years. When the priest entered that flooding river, only then did the waters cease to flow and the Israelites could cross over. We have found this to be true as we have built for the Lord. The majority of our buildings were only partially funded when we began construction. First came the inspiration, then the design, followed by the funding most of which did not materialise until it was needed to continue the construction. Here I will share several stories that illustrate how God has worked to build our faith and

123

build Himself a place where young and old can be discipled, and in turn trained to disciple.

We had already constructed two orphanage duplexes, and these were almost full. The masterplan conceived the construction of eight orphanage duplex buildings as needed, according to the numbers of orphans that would come to us. Now there was a need for the third building. At this point we were feeding around fifty orphans plus paying teachers at the school and orphanage parents in four homes. We were asking God for funds and trusting in His daily provision to keep the growing ministry operational. Our understanding of how God wanted to work with our ministry was ever growing. We were learning to live by faith and build by faith. With a donation toward the new orphanage building we began work knowing the money was only a part of the total needed. The building progressed to where we needed to put the roof on and the doors and windows in. The quotation for construction of the roof, doors and windows was $8500. In hand we had a total of $4500 which was needed for operation as well as construction. In faith we contracted the builder and gave him $4500 with the understanding the remaining $4000 would be paid on the completion of the project. Work progressed slowly as the builder would often take his men to work on other projects. From me, there was no complaint, as I knew I did not have the money to pay him for completing the project. Finally the day came when the project would be completed and the $4000 would be due. I learned that day that God wanted to teach me to trust Him implicitly. It was the same day work was completed that $5000 came into our bank account. The contractor was paid in full and there was money for feeding orphans and paying wages. I later learned that an unknown donor in Iceland had learned about the work we were doing from someone we had not met and had sent the money about three months before its arrival. The money took its time to reach us, but arrived at exactly the right time to teach me that God knows our need and when best to meet that need.

In 2009 we had felt impressed that it was time to move forward with our ministry work by constructing a television studio. We were living by faith, daily dependent on God's provision. By this time we had learned that it was not necessary to know what a project would cost. What was important was knowing that God was behind the project. Our son Caleb a student in Australia at that time, living on Australian government student aid, sent us a donation of $200 and said this was for the new studio building. I understood his donation as a sign that it was God's time to start construction. The studio building is 14 meters by 26 meters. So $200 was not going to go far on a building that needed to be sound proof, as planes flying out of the Siem Reap International Airport flew directly over the top of the building. For many years God had been patiently teaching us the lesson that we need to live and work by faith, trusting Him to provide. Now we had opportunity to see how much we trusted God. With $200 in hand the builders were called and construction began. God provided until the walls were completed. But there was no floor and no roof to span this large building. The grass grew inside the shell of a building and I wondered why God had seen fit to bring us thus far and allow things to stop. I remember sitting in the middle of the shell of a building on a moonlit night and talking to God about what had gone wrong. God had told us not to ask anybody for money, to just trust Him, we had been doing that and the blessings had been coming, but now God apparently was holding back the blessing and I did not understand. That night I heard only the sound of crickets and frogs, nothing from God. The lesson I still needed to learn was to trust God even when He appeared to have failed us. God does not always choose to reveal His plans, often letting us wait on Him in faith.

A short time later we received word from the Avondale High School that they would like to bring a group of school leavers to Cambodia to do a service project at Wat Preah Yesu. They had a budget for the project, enough to pour the concrete slab in the studio room and paint the walls on the outside. They accepted the project and arrived late 2009. In planning for their coming, I realised I needed someone who spoke English to coordinate the concrete pour, God already had a plan. Leroy Sharon, the father of Andrew Sharon, one of our American volunteers, was headed for Cambodia and had the necessary construction skills needed to lead the team of students. God's silent planning in the background is something we all need to learn to trust. At the end of the service project as I listened to the testimonies of the high school leavers, I understood the delay in the studio construction. God had a work He wanted to do in the hearts of those students and that work could only be done by pushing the students to give their all as a team to make the project a success. But God also wanted those same students to see Him work a miracle of provision. While the students were still working, I was handed US$10,000 for the roof of the building. I had talked to the students about trusting God to provide and without my solicitation they witnessed God's provision. The steel for the roof was delivered before the students returned to Australia. I believe the delay in construction was not a delay at all, rather a well-timed strategic move of God's for the salvation of souls.

126

This building needed steel trusses that could span 14 meters to hold the heavy roof up. We had welders on our staff but not the expertise to design and weld these trusses. Again God had everything prepared ahead of time. Leroy Sharon by trade was a steel fabricator, and he built the first truss teaching our staff how to construct the rest of the trusses.

It took about 15 months with God's planned delay to finish the studio building. I had learned that even the ceasing of provision can have a God given purpose. The final cost of the building was very close to US$70,000. We had begun with US$200 and God had miraculously provided the rest. By August 2010, we had a large building, one camera, one iMac computer, one microphone and three smart tech savvy year 11 drop outs as our media team, one of those young men being our youngest son Shannon. At that time a Canadian businessman contacted me to see how he could help our ministry. I shared with him our media project and he generously funded equipment for the project. Together with another unsolicited donation from Australia of AU$20,000, we were able to outfit our studio building with equipment and begin the multi-media venture.

When Joshua and the people of Israel walked into the promised land of Canaan, it appeared to be an impossibility. God's command was go forward.

Do Anything Including Media Ministry

At the very beginning of the 21st century, we began to look at how we could use media to share the gospel more quickly in this Buddhist nation. Radio and television were both politically and financially out of the question. We decided to start with what could be obtained locally that being second hand cassette copiers and recorders. An investment of around US$200 set us up with two cassette copying machines and a cassette recorder. Lessons were developed and recorded in the Khmer language and copies passed around. It was a humble beginning and we have no idea of what impact it had on the Kingdom of Heaven, but it was a foot into media ministry. Then in 2003, my new friend and lecturer at Pacific Union College, Jon Wood, sent a media student to Cambodia to make a documentary of the work we were doing. Caleb, our oldest son, and I spent a lot of time looking over Jeremy's shoulder as he edited the video he had shot. We both came to the same conclusion, we do not need to go to university for four years to learn how to shoot and edit video. God was sharing His vision to us, it would be many years before that vision would be realised, but God had planted a seed, an idea that would one day become Sangkem Media.

If we were to do multi-media ministry, our students needed to learn how to use computers as this skill would be essential for learning how to edit videos. Second hand computers were purchased. For each grade 8 computer class the students would get the PC, keyboard, monitor and mouse from the storeroom and set them up on their desk before they could begin learning. The first class was a disaster, with only one power outlet in the room, we daisy chained extension leads together to power up our twenty computers. The command was given to switch on the computers, immediately we smelt plastic burning as the extension cable that led to the one plug on the wall melted down. That was the end of that class for that day. An important lesson had been learned by all about how not to overload electrical leads. The next computer class was actually an electricians class with the students helping install a circuit breaker, wires and electrical outlets around the room. The following computer class was a success and the video media ministry had its humble beginning with how to turn on a computer and open Word. Years passed and Marshall Smith, a friend living in Japan, sent us a semi-professional video camera to practice with. In 2008 our senior class began learning the use of a video camera and how to do basic editing. The senior class in 2009 was year 11, the first class to learn TV production. I downloaded a series of modules on TV production, studied them and taught them one at a time. That same year Jon Wood, now president of Jesus for Asia, was about to build a studio in Chiangmai, Thailand. I travelled to meet him and the architect and brought back the plans. Caleb was at this time in Australia studying.

Our first video technicians were our youngest son Shannon and two of his Khmer friends from school. Their job description included spending as much time as necessary on the internet learning how to make professional quality videos and then to pass that information on. The internet and electricity were additional miracles that God had long planned for. While we were building the studio the government was building a sewerage treatment plant about two kilometres south of our property. The sewerage treatment plant required stable electricity and fibre optic internet. In 2010 it was pretty much unheard of to have fibre optic internet connection in the countryside and at that time the nearest electrical poles were about five kilometres away in the town. But the construction of the sewerage plant changed our neighbourhood, providing homes with electricity. The villages between ours and town did not immediately have this luxury. The internet provider to the sewerage treatment plant set us up with high speed internet via fibre optic cable for just US$75 installation fee. The electricity connection required a donation of US$15,000 to put in 800 metres of heavy duty three phase wire and the poles to hold it. God's abundant provision left us with no doubt that the media ministry was His plan and in various ways He had made provision for it.

Today Sangkem Media has a media team of nine, plus students who help with production during their vocational work time. The media team teach a subject on multimedia to our grade eleven students, who also help with video production as a part of their course, and a photography class to grade 10. Sangkem Media has seven YouTube channels, a Facebook page, a 24/7 online TV channel and an App called Sangkem (hope), the latter giving people easy access to media produced by Sangkem Media, Hope Cambodia, the Cambodia Adventist Mission and local churches. The media team also broadcast our Sabbath worship program live every week, with more viewers than there are Adventist members in Cambodia. They also work on the translation of Christian books into the Khmer language.

What began as a humble cassette ministry is now reaching Khmer speaking people all over the world. God had a dream and little by little shared that dream with us, blessing as we walked in faith with Him to make His dream a reality. By faith Sangkem Media continues to operate, by faith equipment is replaced and upgraded, by faith we venture into new areas of media ministry to maximise the Gospel impact for the Kingdom of Heaven.

God had a dream and little by little shared that dream with us, blessing as we walked in faith with Him to make His dream a reality.

Butterfly Paradise

(Me) Hi Dani, How are you today? (Dani) Tim, "I have idea for you. Tourists are looking for things to do in the spare hours they have while visiting Siem Reap. You have lots of land and are close to the city, why don't you build a butterfly garden where tourists can come and relax?"

That was part of a conversation between my friend Dani Jump and I, back in July 2014. Neither Dani nor I realised what God had in mind when He impressed Dani to make this suggestion.

Dani had helped with setting out gardens for two butterfly attractions in Cambodia. I had taken my children to butterfly attractions in Thailand, Malaysia and Singapore, and caught butterflies with them around the Angkor Wat temple complex. Neither of us were qualified to establish a tourist attraction featuring butterflies.

I had been looking for an industry that would help our ministry to be self-supporting, but the only industry that was making money, apart from real estate, was tourism. Venturing into tourism and real estate were not the kind of business ventures I was looking for. Dani had proposed a tourism venture.

The first angel's message of Revelation 14 calls people to worship the Creator. Highlighting the design in nature to tourists visiting the attraction would create an urban centre of influence while generating income, and providing work experience to the young people coming through our school. I was seeing the possibilities but already working full-time, and our ministry was operating financially by faith from day to day. Such an investment seemed unwise, but I discussed it with God, recognising a history of poor insight with regard to God's will. The idea was like a seed but it had not germinated until one afternoon after I met with two visiting Adventist businessmen in Siem Reap town. I drove home unusually slowly that afternoon tossing around in my head the possibilities. By the time I reached home I was almost sold on the idea but still had my doubts. Siem Reap already had a small butterfly garden for tourists, it was a long way out of town and kind of rustic in the way it was set up. If we were going to invite tourist to see butterflies, the presentation had to be first class in order to honour the Creator. The more I thought about it, the bigger the project grew in my mind. I began to get seriously nervous about the complexity and size of what I was seeing, not to mention the cost. Faith based living is great because budgets are not required as we are working with God on His projects. But this time I was looking for an excuse to talk God out of this project so I worked on a budget, which came in around US$360,000. It was not long until the proposed budget had risen to US$400,000. This was five times larger than any single project we had done and we were running our ministry on what God provided each day. I tried hard to convince God that it would cost too much, that I did not have the time to invest in it, that Jesus was coming soon so it would not have the intended impact. All I heard was, 'get started'. I asked if I could crowd source the project as the profit would provide for the orphans and schools, things that people like to donate to. The answer was a clear no. I resigned myself to the fact that God was in charge, consoling myself with the fact that all the previous projects God had asked us to do were completed and operating so God could do it again if it was His will.

I worked on a business plan, running through the figures. At the time, Siem Reap was receiving three million visitors a year. If thirty thousand of these visited the butterfly garden each year, we could fully fund all our projects and have money to help fund Cambodia Adventist Mission projects. Evangelism began to be a secondary goal and money making a primary goal.

My late mother Maureen was the first donor, giving the money needed to land fill the rice field where the project would be constructed. While waiting to see what God would do, we began upgrading the school's little plant nursery into a nursery that could propagate thousands of plants. I also became an avid plant collector not only in country but also in other countries when I was traveling.

In my mind Butterfly Paradise had become a reality. With the landfill completed, we needed plans on paper that builders could follow. I took a large sheet of white paper, laid it on the kitchen bench, told God about the paper and asked to see His design by morning. I arose early the next morning expectant to see God's masterpiece of design. When I saw the paper was still blank, I was disappointed, my faith had crossed a boundary into presumption. During my morning devotional time, I took the problem to God and was reproved with the words, 'I gave you a brain, use it. I will help you.' With the promise of God's help to design one of the largest butterfly enclosures in the world, I began designing drainage, pathways, irrigation, 3-phase electrical layout, ponds, waterfalls, buildings and the structural support frame and tensioned wires for a cage 2400 of square metres .

Then our first big donation came, as a clear sign God was behind this project. A friend of a friend heard about the work our ministry was doing in Cambodia and felt impressed by the Holy Spirit to sell his apartment and donate the funds to help provide for the long term care of the orphans, this being one of the key motives for building Butterfly Paradise. Over the next couple of years our builders, all from the local villages, worked hard to turn a dream into a reality. Creativity was a mandatory requirement for the builders. I wanted every feature in the garden to look as natural as possible. This required turning our cage support poles into leafless trees, creating caves that look like rock and waterfalls that could have been found in the forest. Early on in this work, I realised our builders had a problem. Of the four main builders only one had ever seen a rock larger than what they use in foundation construction. I called work off for the morning and drove the builders out to our camp ground and led them into the forest to study large rocks. We studied texture, colour, shape, all the while discussing how they were going to reproduce what they were seeing. On their return, they began experimenting until they perfected using cement to recreate rocks that looked like the ones in the forest.

I have learned that what I see in my head does not have to be the final product. To this end I would vision cast to the builders what could be and then let them construct what they perceived I was seeing. This took a lot of the stress out of the finishing process. The other de-stressor was keeping the end product in mind rather than the method to get there. One of the master pieces these men achieved was the construction of the world's largest concrete caterpillar at the entrance to the garden. Working for the Lord should be fun and these non-Christian tradesmen had a lot of fun while building paradise.

As construction was entering its second year, we faced a faith challenge. Many of our builders lived from one pay to the next. If I did not pay them on time their families did not eat. Pay day came around and it was three o'clock in the afternoon when I began a discussion with God that went something like this; "God we have no money to pay the builders, if you don't send the money before five I will have to tell them to go find other work." An hour later I answered a knock on the door and received $500 from a visitor, just the amount I needed to pay the builders. A month later I was having a repeat conversation with God about the finances and the builders. One hour later I answered another knock on the door and received $600 from a different visitor. Only God and I knew about these immediate needs. After this second very timely miracle, I promised God we would just keep building until the building was done. I had understood His silent message.

In the visions of my head, I saw the Butterfly Paradise restaurant having murals of butterflies and scenery on the walls. God must have planted this vision and was already at work on providing the muralist. This is how I remember the story. David Sauer, a semi-retired muralist was attending ASI USA. While visiting the many booths, he felt tired and sat down on a chair in an empty unmarked booth. Daniel Dreher happened to be passing this empty booth when he saw a sign behind David saying Muralist for Jesus. As Daniel was looking for a muralist for a project in Thailand, he visited with David and signed him up for some artwork in Bangkok. Did you catch the miracle? David had sat down in an empty unmarked booth, and Daniel saw a sign that did not exist. While working on the mural in Thailand David had to leave the country for a few days in order to renew his visa. Daniel brought David to visit with us, which resulted in large beautiful murals of butterflies and caterpillars gracing the walls of the restaurant. Never underestimate God's ability to provide the right people at the right time.

Butterfly Paradise opened on December 25, 2018. Five years have passed, and Butterfly Paradise has never yet had a month when it has broken even. Covid did not help that situation, bringing tourism in Siem Reap to a complete stop which included the closure of the international airport and the border crossings into neighbouring countries. God has taught me that Butterfly Paradise was never about making money, even if that was what I thought. Butterfly Paradise is about introducing people to their Creator through the complexity of design in nature and particularly the butterfly. The cinema airs video shorts that highlight this design and introduce the visitors to the evidence for a loving Creator. The restaurant offers food that promotes health based on biblical principles, spiritual brochures are available in the gift shop, and God arranges divine appointments with guests that give us and our staff opportunities to tell of God's love expressed through design, and so much more. Butterfly Paradise opens its doors Sunday to Friday as a testimony that God is a dreamer of what could be, if His people will partner with Him in making His dreams come true.

Anywhere - International Speaker

When Wendy and I signed up for mission with God, we were not public speakers. Yes we would stand in front of a church and speak, but it was not something we did for the joy of testifying to God's goodness, rather something done with fear and trepidation. Over time as we have drawn nearer to the heart of God, our hearts have changed to where testifying of His goodness is something we love to do. God has given us a testimony, and through the experiences of partnering with Him in mission has also given us interesting insights into scripture and the relationship God desires to have with us on a daily basis.

In 2008, Jon Wood, president of Jesus For Asia, invited Wendy and me to testify to God's goodness at a Faith Camp in Idaho, USA. As faith-based volunteer missionaries who expended all our savings in establishing the work God called us to, we have no money for travel but God sees that as His opportunity. Jesus For Asia offered to pay our airfares, but I believed I was hearing the Holy Spirit say it was easier for God to send me the money directly than to send it to Jesus for Asia and them to send it to us, so we accepted the speaking invitation and declined the airfare. Only days later we noticed a donation for AU$6500 in our bank account and enquired of the giver what purpose he had in mind for this money. To our surprise, he said the gift was conditional and had to be used for ourselves. We asked him if spending it on travel to the USA for Wendy, Shannon and me met his requirements, to which his reply was yes. God used this opportunity to teach us that if we will testify for Him, He will provide the opportunities and the means to give our testimony.

138

Since we began this walk of faith we have travelled more than we ever travelled when we had a salary. God has called me to glorify Him in Taiwan, Philippines, Malaysia, Laos, Thailand, Indonesia, Timor Leste, Germany, USA, and Australia. Via Zoom I have spoken in other countries and people from other countries have come here to hear us give a testimony of God's goodness.

The fear of public speaking has been replaced with joy and expectation of what words God will put in our mouths to bring glory to Him. We continue to be amazed at how God has honoured us as we honour Him. People can argue against a religious teaching, but it is hard for them to argue against the testimony of one who was on the scene experiencing the power of God at work.

When God is enthroned as Lord of our lives, we can do all things as we draw on His strength, wisdom and love. His presence banishes fear and makes us bold for His honour.

People can argue against a religious teaching, but it is hard for them to argue against the testimony of one who was on the scene experiencing the power of God at work.

Dreaming Together with God

One example of God dreaming for me began one Sabbath afternoon during a Pathfinder camp at Thmor Chol Village. The simple Seventh-day Adventist Church in this village is opposite the Kulen Mountain National Park. Between the church and boundary of the national park are two blocks of land with a permanent stream running between them. We often hiked the Pathfinders up the mountain to camp for four to five days, but on this occasion we were camping around the church. I was sitting on the sandy road running down to the stream, looking at the burned over piece of land that adjoined the national park. There was nothing about this barren piece of land that appealed to me, but as I sat there looking, I heard the Holy Spirit tell me that I was to buy the charred land for a camp ground and the land I was sitting on for a Lifestyle centre. Neither of these projects were on our ministry dream list. The impression was so strong, the next day I asked a church member from the village if he knew whether the charred land was for sale. He enquired and it was not for sale. I understood from him that the boundary for the national park was not clear meaning the land could be in the national park. It sounded hopeless but I had heard God say buy it. I forgot to mention another problem, we had no money for purchasing land. The piece of land I was sitting on belonged to a church member but at the time they had no intention of selling as they were using the land to support themselves.

I clung to God's dream. Time passed and I trusted that God had everything under control. This land is 50 km from Siem Reap city. Land owners in the countryside did not have land titles recognised at provincial government level. But God was at work, and for reasons still unknown to us, apart from the fact that God was at work, the lands department went out to Thmor Chol village and issued everyone official land titles, skipping all the villages in between. Now both pieces of land were titled and the boundary of the national park was fixed. Two apparent problems continued, the owners did not want to sell and we had no money. I understood my part was not to get discouraged or give up hope. My part was to keep looking to God with the end goal in mind. I could not see what God was doing behind the scenes but trusted He had everything under control. Then the second and third miracle happened hours apart. I learned that we had US$40,000 coming to our ministry from a deceased estate and we were free to decide how to use the money. Within hours I was told the land owners wife was seriously ill and he needed money to take her to Thailand for treatment and had decided to sell the charred land. When I went to pick up the land title from the owner, I was surprised to watch him sorting through a stack of land titles for the one that adjoined the national park. I saw God had worked yet another miracle. This man was the wealthiest landowner in that area and of all the land he owned, He decided to sell the piece that God wanted us to buy.

The second piece of land was purchased after Marienhöhe School asked us for a project they could sponsor and we suggested money to purchase the land for the future health retreat. By this time the owners of that high land had decided they wanted to buy low land for growing rice, with this the land exchanged owners, with the Cambodia Adventist Mission corporation becoming the new land owner. Our ministry policy has always been that all land purchased with donation money should be owned by the Cambodia Adventist Mission, our role is to develop the land for the glory of God on behalf of the Mission.

Today the formerly charred land adjoining the national park is a beautiful park, with bathrooms, and a large covered meeting area, where Pathfinders, youth and church members can experience God through being close to nature. The land for the Lifestyle Centre has sat idle waiting on God's timing, but as I write God appears to be opening the way for the rich suffering from lifestyle diseases, to receive their invitation to the Kingdom of Heaven.

More than ten years have passed since God told me about this dream. By partnering with God, we and others are making His dream our reality.

After 28 years of faith-based living, we have learned that God is thinking ahead for His people. This is comforting, knowing that we do not know the future, but He does. We have learned through experience, that our part is to partner with God in dreaming what could be if....

Maybe you are wondering why I never finished that last sentence. Let me explain. God has all knowledge, power, and wisdom in heaven and on earth. There is nothing stopping God turning His dreams into reality except you or me if we are the active earthly agents of change in that dream. If we hesitate, or worse still, refuse to partner with Him in making His dream for us a reality we hinder the work of God.

Now let me finish the sentence. My part is to partner with God in dreaming what could be if I trust Him absolutely (zero doubt), working with Him to make our dream come true. Paul touched on this in Hebrews 11:1, "Now faith is the substance of things hoped for, the evidence of things not seen." When we focus on God with the end goal in mind, we won't doubt, wondering how we will reach that goal. It would be a whole lot easier for God to just speak His dream into existence. At creation He proved that is His reality. But God wants us to partner in creating with Him, doing what seems impossible. Through these experiences with God, we begin to understand what it is to have the faith of Jesus. Jesus' mission here on earth was impossible. He was to live in a man's body with a man's power and overcome Satan. This had never been done in the previous four thousand years of Earth's history, so why did Jesus think He could be successful? Number one, He knew the Father. Secondly, He knew that while He had divested Himself of His power, through the mystery of the indwelling presence of the Holy Spirit, the Father dwelt within Him, and through the Father's power, victory would be His. Jesus realised victory is the product of absolute surrender. The Faith of Jesus is having absolute trust in the Godhead, knowing that if I have died to self and Christ lives in me, I have the same power that was working in Jesus working in me. The victory Jesus gained is mine all the time that I am His.

My part is to partner with God in dreaming what could be if I trust Him absolutely (zero doubt), working with Him to make our dream come true.

Any Cost - When Sacrifice Is Gain

In 1984, when Wendy and I promised God that we would go anywhere, do anything, for any length of time, we had no idea what that would cost us. We had read the mission stories where the servant of God or members of the family were buried in foreign soil or at sea. True surrender does not count the cost. We began our journey straight out of university with no money and no debts. Thirty-nine years later we still have no money and no debts, so nothing changed there. We began as a couple and now have two grown children of our own and an adopted daughter and six grandchildren, all in good health and living on the same campus as us, contributing to the same mission. Here I see only gain.

Hundreds know God and are awaiting the coming of Jesus because we said, "We will go." As we have discipled others, we ourselves have become true disciples under the discipleship of the Holy Spirit. Jesus is no longer an add-on to our lives, He is at the very centre of everything we do. His love for people, has become our love for people. His Joy is our joy, His peace our peace.

We wake up each day with the expectation of partnering with God in ministry for those less fortunate. I cannot think of a better reason for going to work each day. For this reason we maintain the very best health possible by eating a simple, whole food plant based diet, and joyously living the rest of the eight laws of health. There is sacrifice here, but it does not compare with the gain.

We have seen the miracle of God fulfilling His promise in Matthew 6:33, that if we would seek the (good of the)

Kingdom of Heaven and His righteousness, all these other things would be added. We have learned the reality of the joy Jesus promised as we have partnered together with Him. We bask in the peace that knows no understanding, knowing that all heaven is on our side. We look forward to the time of trouble with expectation, having already seen God come through for us today.

Yes, there has been pain from illness, accidents, exhaustion and burnout. Yes, we have spent days, weeks and months with sweat running down our bodies from morning to night. Yes, there have been times when we have had to deny ourselves so that we would not have to deny another. That all seems so inconsequential in comparison to the joy of seeing souls saved into the Kingdom of God.

God's call to service often does not involve a lifetime in a foreign land. God's call to service often comes with the cost of what the world would call financial loss. God's call to service is to take up our cross and unite with Him in an eternal journey beginning today. We long for the second coming of Jesus, while Jesus longs for us to accompany Him everyday in ministering to others. Matthew chose to close out Jesus' words by writing, "All power is given unto me in heaven and in earth. Go ye therefore, and teach all nations, baptising them in the name of the Father, and of the Son, and of the Holy Ghost: Teaching them to observe all things whatsoever I have commanded you: and, lo, I am with you alway, even unto the end of the world" (Matthew 28:18-20). The mystery of God is that when we are involved in disciple making, Jesus is right here in us. Why wait for heaven to be with Jesus when you can partner with Him in mission today?

It is our hope that these stories have inspired you in the same way Wendy and I were inspired by mission stories 40 years ago. Jesus' encouragement to His disciples to pray for more workers as the fields are ripe, is even more urgent today. If you will join us by going to your knees, whole heartedly promising God you will go anywhere, do anything, for any length of time at any cost, you to can begin a journey with Jesus. Jesus is recruiting the 144,000 to finish His work in righteousness. Be one of those who daily choose to accompany the Lamb wherever He goes. Don't wait for heaven, reign together with Jesus today.

Silver and gold we have none, but what we have we give to you: in the name of Jesus, rise up and minister to the lost. Not for the reward of being able to boast about the sacrifice you made, nor because you think it will get you to heaven, or because you want to travel to exotic foreign countries, but simply because Jesus asked you to accompany Him daily in ministering to His children, some of whom will become your treasure in heaven. Here is true Joy.

We long for the second coming of Jesus, while Jesus longs for us to accompany Him today in ministering to others.

To contact the author   tim@saltmin.org

Seventh-day Adventist church Identities and Mission sending Organisations

Adventist Mission   adventistmission.org

Church Volunteer Positions   vividfaith.com

Jesus For Asia   jesus4asia.org

ASAP Ministries   asapministries.org

Adventist Frontier Missions   afmonline.org

Outpost Centers International   outpostcenters.org

Laymen Ministries   lmn.org

Made in United States
Troutdale, OR
09/26/2024

23153039R00089